The current social media climate of  mom feeling less-than when she com_____ moms. But what if we learned to actual_____ ...perfect parts of our days as we parent our kids ... the midst of the mess that motherhood often is? *The Bet___ Mom* is a fresh dose of perspective that will enable moms to grow i_ _ce, find God in the small things, and learn to love their lives.

KAREN EHMAN, Proverbs 31 Ministries speaker
and *New York Times* bestselling author
of *Keep It Shut* and *Pressing Pause*

This book is a cup of cold water for the endurance run of being a mom. Whether you've just begun or you are fifteen or twenty years along that road—your soul needs this water stop. Her words refreshed my motherhood.

SARA HAGERTY, author of *Unseen* and *Every*
Bitter Thing is Sweet

Who knew motherhood was supposed to be messy? The perfect combination of encouragement and inspiration, *The Better Mom* is the perfect dose of reality and grace for any mom feeling like they've fallen short.

RUTH SOUKUP, *New York Times* bestselling
author of *Living Well, Spending Less*

The Better Mom is the perfect encouragement for every mom's heart! Through vulnerability and sharing personal stories of her own motherhood journey, Ruth inspires moms to intentionally pursue becoming better moms as we all seek to be more like Christ. Ruth's stories of motherhood and marriage are relatable, letting us know that none of us are really alone in our struggles. *The Better Mom* reminds us not to idolize perfection and experience the discouragement of failure, but rather embrace the truth that we can continue to be better as we grow and mature in our own motherhood journeys.

JENNIFER SMITH, author of *The Unveiled*
Wife and *Wife After God*

Ruth's newest book will give you a counselor to listen to, a friend to walk beside you, and an experienced voice from someone who has learned to seek God's grace and truth every step of motherhood. Love this book.

SALLY CLARKSON, speaker, blogger, podcaster, and author
of numerous bestselling books, including *The Mission
of Motherhood*, *Desperate*, and *The Lifegiving Home*

I have spent the last eighteen years of parenting working toward being a better mom. I wish I'd had this book years ago! I think every mother would benefit from reading *The Better Mom*. It's honest, insightful, and so encouraging!

KRISTEN WELCH, bestselling author of *Raising
Grateful Kids in An Entitled World*

Ruth Schwenk is an ambassador for us moms in the trenches. She knows the worries that weigh heavily on our hearts, and she gets the mom guilt that threatens to steal the joy from our parenting journeys. And she is passionate about helping us grow *through* it and find freedom *in* it. The Better Mom is a beautiful invitation to draw nearer to the heart of God where he shapes us more into his likeness and we therefore become more of who we long to be for our kids.

JEANNIE CUNNION, author of *Mom Set Free*

The Better Mom is a breath of fresh air for moms who deeply care to get it right, and sometimes perfect. The great irony of this book is that Ruth invites all the do-ers to do less, and thus experience more during the demanding momming years. A fantastic and encouraging read!

COURTNEY DEFEO, speaker and author
of *In This House, We Will Giggle*

Motherhood is a journey, and *The Better Mom* is the perfect guide for this journey. Ruth's transparency reminds me that I am not alone and that my discouragements and struggles are normal. She is so real! Ruth intertwines her life experience and stories with Scripture in a profound way, as she reminds us that God is shaping us as we are shaping our children. This is a must read for all moms, in all walks of life.

COURTNEY JOSEPH, author and blogger at
WomenLivingWell.org, home of Good Morning Girls

Got kids? If so, you need Ruth Schwenk's newest book, titled after her popular blog *The Better Mom*. I've noticed that we're living in a culture that tends toward extremes—and motherhood is no exception. In her book, Ruth gently calls moms back to a place of biblically based, Christ-honoring balance in everything from creating a God-honoring home to overcoming unhealthy habits in parenting.

HEIDI ST. JOHN, MomStrong International, author, speaker,
blogger, and executive director at Firmly Planted Family

In a culture filled with mom wars and mom guilt, Ruth Schwenk offers a gentle invitation to a grace-filled alternative in *The Better Mom*. Rife with encouragement and spiritual application, this book will spur readers on to give God glory through our momming, even in the mess.

ERIN ODOM, author of *More Than Just Making It* and *You Can Stay
Home with Your Kids* and creator of *The Humbled Homemaker* blog

Half the time I feel like *a worn mom, a burdened mom* or a *wrestling-with-discipline mom*. I wonder if I am really cut out for this job. Ruth Schwenk's book, *The Better Mom*, is the encouragement us weary moms need. With great authenticity, she shows us that our worth is greater than our wavering feelings and our value reaches far beyond the endless mistakes we constantly seem to make. If you need hope for today, and for your future, this book is for you.

KELLY BALARIE, speaker, author of *Fear Fighting* and
Battle Ready, and blogger at www.purposefulfaith.com

This book will revolutionize the way you see motherhood. You'll be reminded of your high and worthwhile calling. Ruth writes with grace, humor, and wisdom, giving you the tools necessary to succeed as a mom. As a mom in the trenches herself, Ruth gets it!

ARLENE PELLICANE, speaker and author of *Parents Rising*

OTHER BOOKS BY RUTH SCHWENK

For Better or For Kids (with Patrick Schwenk)

Hoodwinked (with Karen Ehman)

Pressing Pause (with Karen Ehman)

the better mom

GROWING IN GRACE BETWEEN *perfection* and the MESS

RUTH SCHWENK

ZONDERVAN®

ZONDERVAN

The Better Mom
Copyright © 2018 by Ruth Schwenk

Requests for information should be addressed to:
Zondervan, *3900 Sparks Dr. SE, Grand Rapids, Michigan 49546*

ISBN 978-0-310-34945-7 (softcover)

ISBN 978-0-310-35313-3 (audio)

ISBN 978-0-310-34946-4 (ebook)

Published in association with The Fedd Agency, P.O. Box 341973, Austin, TX 78734.

Cover art: Juicebox Designs
Interior design: Denise Froehlich

First printing February 2018/Printed in the United States of America

To Tyler, Bella, Noah, and Sophia
God blessed me beyond measure when
he gave me each of you.

Contents

CHAPTER I

This Is What I Signed Up For?

"Wait a second. Are you saying *you* are the better mom?" My son's friend had overheard my husband and me talking about my website, *The Better Mom*, and he couldn't contain his curiosity any longer. Perhaps in defense of his own mom, he spoke again. "So, are you saying you are better than any of the other moms in the neighborhood?"

I couldn't help but laugh out loud as I explained to him that *The Better Mom* isn't about me, Ruth Schwenk, being *the* better mom. *The Better Mom* is a community, a place where moms can gather online to learn and grow together. It's a whole lot of moms who don't think they *are* better, but who *want* to be better.

The Better Mom is about us. It's about you. It's about the countless moms from all different walks of life, in different seasons, and literally from all around the world. It's about moms who want to be better at this glorious and grueling calling of momming.

There is no greater joy than being a wife and a mother. I have been married to my pastor-husband, Patrick, for nearly twenty years, and we have four amazing kids whom I love to pieces. Tyler is our easygoing and gentle-hearted son. He has a quiet confidence that causes him to be fearless. He reminds me to be bold and sometimes just "go for it!" Bella, our oldest daughter, loves to give. She has shown me the value of serving—surprising others with small acts of selfless love. Noah keeps us laughing with his one-liners. As our resident comedian, he has taught me to never take life (or myself) too seriously. And Sophia, who has a vivid imagination and extra-large personality, wakes up every day as if it is the best day of her life! She is always enthusiastic about life and keeps me hoping, learning, and dreaming.

I love being a wife and a mom. I bet you do too. But no matter how much we love being moms, inevitably something will happen, and the deepest heart-cries boiling inside us will burst into full view:

"I have no idea what I'm doing!"

"I hate this stage of life."

"I miss my friends."

"Everything depends on me."

When we encounter the deepest cries of our momming hearts, we are getting closer to understanding the secret of *The Better Mom*. Want to know what it is? The secret to being a better mom? It's probably different than you think.

The Better Mom isn't just about how to raise your kids, make picture-worthy crafts, save money, cook nutritious meals, or throw great birthday parties. *The Better Mom* is about something far bigger. Far better. *The Better Mom* is not just about what *we* are doing; it's about what *God* is doing in us. It is who God is inviting us to become in the process.

As a mom it can be tempting to glorify the mess. And just as tempting is the desire to idolize perfection. Both are unhealthy extremes. This is a book about how God is molding and shaping our character, growing us in grace between perfection and the mess. God is inviting us to *be* and *become* better, more like Christ, not just to *do* better.

We don't have to have too many miles behind us in this momming journey to discover our need for heart-change. For me, it started before I was even a mom.

A FAR CRY FROM BABY DOLLS

After a bit of wrangling, the Pack 'n Play was all set up. I stepped back to admire my work. A handful of toys. Some picture books. A cuddly blanket. A swing. I gave the baby swing a soft push and let it rock back and forth to the soothing tune of "Twinkle, Twinkle, Little Star."

"Perfect," I said to myself. My nursery didn't have an occupant yet, but I knew he was on his way. His parents were due to drop him off at any moment!

My first babysitting job was about to become a reality. It wasn't exactly motherhood, but as a fourteen-year-old, I was excited about practicing to be a mom—something I had dreamed about for as long as I could remember. At that age, my idea of being a mom was pushing a stroller around the park on sunny days. I had visions of picking out clothes, painting a nursery, and snuggling on the couch. I'd envision my kids learning to walk, talking for the first time, and reading books on their own. Like me, they'd love football, enjoy singing, and want to go to musicals.

The doorbell rang, interrupting my pleasant daydreams. The

parents gave me a few instructions and put the little guy into my arms. For a few fleeting hours, he was mine. I read him a few books, transferred him to the swing for a while, gave him a bottle, and then—just like that—his parents were there to pick him up.

Well, that was easy! He never cried, pooped, or really did much at all. I didn't even need to use the Pack 'n Play. I thought I had the momming thing pretty well figured out. It was going to be a cinch!

Those were my first steps in what would prove to be a long journey of truly understanding what it means to be a mom. Almost ten years after that first babysitting job, I set my eyes on my own son for the first time. He was a far cry from the baby dolls I grew up playing with. He was real.

For a long time I gazed at him in wonder. I took in the new baby sounds and smells. I examined his little hands and tiny toes. He was barely seven pounds and could wail with the best of them, but by my estimation he was perfect. Warm and snug, tightly wrapped in his blanket, I held him close to me. The dream of being a mom was finally a reality. It was good.

GOOD IN EVERY WAY

I know I'm not the only mom who had that feeling of deep, contented goodness. It's more than the relief and joy of bringing a son or daughter into the world. It's a sense of wonder at how that baby, another human being, grew inside of me. It's the anticipation, excitement, and appreciation of a new creation. All these emotions are wrapped up in the moment we first lay eyes on our own children.

I so appreciate and understand the story in the Bible of

Moses's mom when she saw her son for the first time. When she saw Moses, "she saw that he was a fine child" (Exodus 2:2). In Hebrew it literally reads, "she saw that he was good." What amazes me is that she uses the same word to describe her newborn son that God used when he saw his creation in Genesis 1. God, too, proclaimed of his new creation, "It is good!"

Like God, we can't help but let it out: our newborn child is *good*! We can't help but take pictures of our kids and post them on every social media outlet. We want to tell the world. It's not enough for us to enjoy our kids; we want the whole world (or at least our followers) to share in the goodness too. But we're not the only ones who delight in our kids.

God loves family. He loves children. He gives them as a gift, entrusting them to us. The goodness of kids is not only that they fulfill us but also that they help fulfill God's purpose in the world. The Bible has plenty to say about the joy and blessing of bringing a son or daughter into the world.

I discovered two powerful words God uses to demonstrate the goodness and blessing of children: *reward* and *arrows* (Psalm 127). Who doesn't like a reward? It's a word that means a wage or payment. I have never met anyone who received a paycheck and felt it was a burden! Children are like a payment we can receive joyfully—and one we must handle wisely.

Not only are children a reward, they are like arrows. Arrows and swords were two primary weapons of warfare in the ancient world. In God's hands, our kids can grow up to fulfill God's purpose of piercing the darkness of the world in which they live—they are like weapons of truth, life, and light in a broken and hurting world.

As moms we have every reason to look at our kids and declare them to be good. But for all the goodness and joy that kids bring, momming may still be one of the most difficult things we ever do. It takes lots of pain, sweat, and tears to bring them *into* the world, and just as much goes into bringing them *up* in the world. All too often our unrealistic visions of what our family life should look like actually add to our growing pains as mothers. We find ourselves wondering, "How could something so good be so hard?"

SHATTERED EXPECTATIONS

I grew up going to my grandparents' house almost every Sunday night. We'd gather for dinner and afterward we would often linger at the table to chat. Other times we'd go for a walk around their neighborhood. Sometimes we worked on a puzzle or played UNO. So when I dreamed of growing up and getting married, building a family, and creating a home, I envisioned family time that was like Grandma's—peaceful and, well, almost perfect.

There was only one problem: Grandma's kids no longer lived at home! I made the mistake of thinking that marriage and building a family was always going to be full of meaning and fun. I envisioned our home being like a visit at Grandma's—filled with game nights, long dinners with meaningful conversations, and lots of family time together. Of course, there was nothing wrong with my dreams of family; they were good—very good—but they weren't the whole picture. They were a far cry from reality, and pretty early on my expectations began to shatter.

As I would find out, reality would invade my peaceful, movie-like visions of being a mom. Many situations would disrupt my expectations of everyday family life. Conversations around the table would sometimes turn into sibling spats. Walks around the neighborhood with four young kids and two dogs looked like the circus coming to town. Quiet evenings working a puzzle were replaced by quick departures from the dinner table—and sometimes the drive-through window—to attend sporting events and extracurricular activities. To top it off, add the challenge of juggling work life and home life, struggles in learning how to parent together, and—of course—loving my spouse with kids in the house. There is pain in childbearing, but the pain of child*rearing* is sometimes greater than we could have dreamed.

The dream of being the mom of a big family, one I defined as having six kids, was shattered by reality too. I endured five heart-wrenching miscarriages, one between the birth of each of our living children and two more after our youngest daughter, Sophia, was born. The doctors never had an answer as to why. My plan of having six children was not going to happen. I knew it was time to surrender that dream.

I don't know how reality may have shattered your dreams and expectations for being a mom, but the truth is, momming is very different from what most of us expect it to be. Who has visions of staying up at night with a sick child? Or dreams of washing and folding what feels like endless loads of laundry? Our dreams of family nights, game times, and meaningful conversations are quickly swallowed up by the mundane and even painful aspects of parenting.

IN OVER OUR HEADS

Did you know the phrase "God will not give you more than you can handle" is not in the Bible? Many people mistakenly believe it is. I lived a lot of years thinking it was too! I have to admit, I wish it were true, because most of us are in way over our heads. It seems we're living with more than we can handle.

We usually don't start out by being in over our heads. But as we add more kids to the mix, the early days of one quiet sleeping baby are replaced with feelings of inadequacy! As our kids grow, our responsibilities change. We might be in tough circumstances, but we certainly are in good company when we feel in over our heads.

I can't help but think of some of the difficulties the people of God faced when he called them to fulfill his purposes. Abraham left his tribal homeland. Moses led Israel out of slavery in Egypt. Esther saved a nation by asking favors of a king who held her life—and the lives of her people—in his hands. Nehemiah left a palace to restore a city in ruins. Noah confronted a corrupt city.

All of it was hard, risky, sacrificial work. But it was the type of work that matters. In every example, God was doing a good work. He was changing lives, redirecting generations, altering outcomes, and restoring what had been destroyed. It was hard work because it mattered. God was accomplishing his purposes, pushing back darkness with his shining light.

Lots of pain, sweat, and tears go into bringing children into the world, and just as much goes into bringing them up in the world.

What I love about each of these stories is not just what God did with these faithful acts of obedience. I love that in every story, the men and women involved were not just used by God, they were forever changed by God. God had given them more than they could handle, but he didn't ask them to handle it alone.

So what if being a mom who seriously wonders how she can handle the mess that is on her plate is exactly where God wants you to be? What if the worn out, scared, exhausted, I-can't-do-this, I-may-need-to-send-the-kids-to-Canada feelings are exactly the place where real transformation begins? What if that is where God wants you to be, but not where he wants you to stay? What if the challenges of being a good mom is God's way of getting your attention so you can focus on being a better mom—God's way?

(RE)STARTING WITH A BETTER QUESTION

Our youngest daughter, Sophia, loves to ask questions. She's almost always the first one awake, so the questions begin early and they don't let up as the day drives on. As much as I love her imagination and inquisitive spirit, being her mom—the person to whom most of those questions are directed—is at times exhausting.

In the middle of a barrage of Sophia questions, when I felt as though I couldn't answer one more, it dawned on me that I tend to ask a lot of questions too. As a mom, I ask questions about sleep, nutrition, schooling, friends . . . and the list goes on. Most of the questions are about what we should be *doing*. These are all good and necessary questions that every mom should be asking. They are necessary, practical, and usually for the well-being of our families (if not for our survival). But in the rush of it all, we often fail to ask one really important question—the question of who we are *becoming*. What is God doing inside me? How is God using the challenges and circumstances of momming to make me more like Christ? How am I allowing him to change me? Who am I becoming?

The work of momming is a high calling. It's full of goodness, adventure, fun, hard work, and sacrifice. Yes, it's messy. Unpredictable. And at times, overwhelming. But the mess is where God wants to meet us. Not to stay there, but to grow there. God is inviting us not to do more, but become more. There is a better way—a way that is more than just feeling tired, overwhelmed, stressed, and ready for it all to be over.

God wants something more for us. He has something more. The way to becoming a better mom starts not with what we are doing, but in asking who God is inviting us to become. When we signed up to become mothers, we thought we were going to get baby giggles and snuggly bedtimes and cozy family dinners. Then we got colicky babies, bedtime battles, and five o'clock "witching" time. But on top of all those things, we got more—so much more. More grace. More growth. More love.

For example, when I became a mother, I fully expected to breastfeed my baby with ease. After all, "breast is best" and the most natural! After a lot of help from the lactation consultant in the hospital, lots of struggling with a rented breast pump, and a few breast infections, I accepted that that particular aspect of motherhood was not going to be anything like I had imagined. I could have beat myself up with this first and dramatically visible momming difficulty. Instead, I comforted myself by remembering other good moms struggle with breastfeeding too. Many have to use formula to supplement their breastfeeding. I learned to embrace and appreciate my new reality.

Can you see what God is doing? Will you look for glimmers of hope, shoots of new growth, even in the midst of the mess of momming? Have you experienced the exhilarating joy of growing in grace, feeling God stretching you and empowering you and working in and through you as a mother? If so, the next time you experience a mothering challenge, perhaps instead of crying, "*This* is what I signed up for?", you'll grab for the nearest pen and declare, "Tell me where to sign up!"

CHAPTER 2

I Have No Idea What I'm Doing!

hen we saw her at the hospital, she was ecstatic. She had endured nine months of doctor appointments, ultrasounds, food cravings, pregnancy scares, growing body parts, swollen ankles, and a whole lot of discomfort. But during the early hours of that morning, she and her husband welcomed their first baby into the world. Finally, her perfect baby girl was born.

But how quickly the euphoria disappears when reality sets in! When we saw her, this new momma was happy and peacefully content, but in less than twenty-four hours, she and her husband would be on their way home—as a family of three. There is something surreal about the moment when the hospital doors open and release you and your new family into the "real world." The mixture of emotions can be overwhelming. One part of you feels joy and the other part absolute fear!

"Now what?"

"No more nurses, doctors?"

"This human being is ours to raise, nurture, protect, and teach?"

"Is it safe to drive?"

"How do we take care of this child?"

"Help!"

During the next few weeks, the mom and I talked and texted a bit. She asked questions about bedtimes, sleeping patterns, breastfeeding, diapers, and ever-changing emotions. It was all new to her, and she was struggling with the questions every mom encounters.

When I saw her and her husband six weeks later, they looked a little spooked. They still glowed with excitement, but they were visibly tired and noticeably nervous about taking their child out of the house. The dad carried their newborn in her car seat that he awkwardly cradled in his arms. The mom carried a diaper bag, extra blankets, a rattle, and a "lovie."

We had been talking for a bit when she finally blurted out, "Ruth, honestly I have no idea what I am doing!" I couldn't help but smile as I reassured her that everything was going to be just fine.

IT'S OKAY TO ADMIT YOU ARE NOT OKAY!

I'll let you in on a little secret. The motherhood gig takes us all a bit by surprise. I had felt the same way my friend did. And most moms, if we are honest, feel that way too. Momming often is not as natural, easy, or instinctive as we think it is supposed to be. So it's okay to admit you don't know what you are doing. It is okay to admit you are not okay.

I know, the small voice in your head is still saying, "Shouldn't I know how to do this?" But that voice is not the voice of truth. So take the pressure off yourself. If anyone tries to judge you, remember that they didn't—and don't—have it all figured out either!

When you think about it, most everything we do in life has to be learned. I spent years figuring out how to cook. Ask my husband! And although I had some natural gifting as a singer, I spent years in vocal training. If you are a mom who also pursues a career, you likely spent years studying, preparing, and gaining the skills you need to succeed.

For the sake of our own hearts, homes, marriages, and families, we need to chase after wisdom.

Momming is no different. We have to pursue the necessary skills and knowledge in order to flourish. Just because we brought a child into the world doesn't mean bringing up that child will come naturally or easily.

The good news is we don't have to limp through life not knowing what to do. We don't have to feel like we are failing. God has given us tremendous resources in his Word and his people. Yes, learning to be a mom takes work. And becoming a better mom is a lifelong commitment. The path isn't always easy, but it is worth it. Unfortunately, for many years, I felt like I was playing catch-up.

WISDOM TAKES WORK, BUT IT IS WORTH IT

I didn't grow up in a Christian home. I didn't attend church on a regular basis and I never went to Sunday school. It wasn't until I was in high school that someone invited me to youth group. Little did I know that accepting that invitation would change my life and my future!

Attending youth group and becoming a Christian altered my college plans. I ended up going to Bible college, something I didn't even know existed until I became a Christian! I had spent a lot of my years living *apart* from God; now I had a new desire to live *with* God. So I did exactly what my youth pastor had told me to do, "Dig into God's Word!"

Much to my surprise, I discovered that everyone is playing catch-up—learning to walk wisely or skillfully doesn't come naturally to anyone. Whether we grew up in a Christian home or not, wisdom—learning to live life God's way—has to be searched for, learned, understood, and then applied. That's why I love the book of Proverbs. So much of it tells us how to find wisdom. Consider, for example, Proverbs 2:1–5:

> My son, if you accept my words
>> and store up my commands within you,
> turning your ear to wisdom
>> and applying your heart to understanding—
> indeed, if you call out for insight
>> and cry aloud for understanding,
> and if you look for it as for silver
>> and search for it as for hidden treasure,
> then you will understand the fear of the LORD
>> and find the knowledge of God.

Did you notice all the action words? Did you see what we must "do" to learn to navigate life well? Figuring out how to do life well in God's way takes accepting God's words, storing up his commands, tuning our ears to his voice, calling out for insight, crying aloud for understanding, and searching for wisdom!

Wisdom takes work! It's not natural. It's not easy. It's not instinctive. Wisdom does not come to us; we have to chase after it. And guess what? There is a reward. Wisdom enables success (Proverbs 2:7). God's truth is like a shield (verse 7). Wisdom can guard and protect us (verse 8). And wisdom can protect us from bad, incorrect, or even sinful counsel from others (verses 12–15).

What does all of this have to do with momming? Everything! When momming doesn't come naturally to us, we need to gain wisdom in those areas. Because we didn't come into the world with everything figured out, we need to do something about it. For the sake of our own hearts, homes, marriages, and families, we need to chase after wisdom. It starts with knowing and understanding who God is and what he desires. The search is worth it!

GAINING WISDOM THROUGH RELATIONSHIPS

Not only does God give us wisdom as we seek him in his Word, he also teaches us wisdom through his people. Those who surround us inevitably shape us, and as we learn to become better moms, God can use relationships in powerful and redemptive ways.

In fact, relationships are one of the primary ways God makes us better, more mature, and ultimately more like Jesus. Think about it for a moment. Can you name the top two or three sermons that most radically changed you? What about the top three songs that have had the most influence in shaping who you are?

This one might be a bit easier, but what about the two or three most life-changing experiences or circumstances? Now how about the two or three people who have impacted you the most? My guess is, as great as sermons, music, circumstances, books, and blogs are, God has used people to help transform your life the most.

During different seasons and for different reasons, God has graciously placed people in my life for my benefit. When we were first married, we were blessed to know a couple who was about ten years ahead of us in life's journey. Not only had they been married much longer, they had a family—a very impressive one. We asked them questions about everything we could think of, soaking up the wisdom God provided through them. Of course, we still had friends in our own stage of life, but we tried to spend time with this godly couple as often as we could. While they are not perfect, we have sought out their wisdom and attempted to pattern our marriage and family after theirs.

Who we follow matters. Just as we are not supposed to listen to everyone, we are not to follow everyone. The New Testament urges us to follow those who are godly and wise followers of Jesus. The apostle Paul was not shy about telling the church to "join together in following my example, brothers and sisters, and just as you have us as a model, keep your eyes on those who live as we do" (Philippians 3:17). His emphasis was on following him *as he followed Christ.*

It takes humility to search for wisdom and listen to others. It is easier to fake it until you make it, but that isn't the path of wisdom. And it's certainly not the path to growth and transformation. The wisdom of Proverbs tells us "the way of fools seems right to them, but the wise listen to advice" (Proverbs 12:15). God has so much for us to learn from other people! As Scripture warns us, when we "stop listening to instruction," we will inevitably "stray from the words of knowledge" (Proverbs 19:27).

We can become better when we make it a priority to reach out to godly moms in our churches, neighborhoods, or communities who we can listen to and learn from. God has placed them in our lives and in the church for a reason. Learn from these women. Gather as much wisdom as you can. Follow their example. Apply what is most true and relevant for your unique family. We all need people to learn from no matter how far along we are in the journey. (For more on this topic, see chapter 14, "I Don't Know Who to Listen To.")

BECOMING A BETTER MOM IS A LIFELONG JOURNEY

I have to confess, I still don't always know what I'm doing. I'm still a mom who is trying to figure it out. I'm still a mom who has to quiet the nagging voice that says, "Shouldn't you know what to do?" And momming will always be that way because just when we think we have figured it out, our kids get a little older, we enter a new season, and the learning begins all over again.

Recently, my husband and I went out to dinner with friends who shared with us some of the struggles they had faced with their high school and college-age children who were grown and out of the house. We ate our food silently, listening intently to every word. Why were their words so important to us? Truth be told, we were in new terrain as parents and were hitting some bumps in the road with our older kids.

Once again we were moving into a different season of life and realizing the road ahead would have some bumps here and there.

We had to admit it's not easy to know how to parent teens. We had to admit we didn't have all the answers and we weren't okay. We were encountering new challenges that were as scary as the ones we faced when we first left the hospital, and we didn't know what to do. We were beginning a new season of learning, and we needed wisdom from those who have gone before us.

Our dinner conversation reminded me that becoming a better mom is a lifelong journey. One season leads to another and to another. Each season is as unique and unfamiliar as the previous one. Each season provides new opportunities for learning, growing, and becoming a better mom.

I don't—and won't—always know what I'm doing. But I know the One who knows me and the road ahead. He is my Father who has promised not to leave me nor forsake me on this journey (Hebrews 13:5). He is a good Father who has shared with me his wisdom, grace, and truth. He is empowering me by his Spirit. In the moments when I doubt I can do this, I can look to him—the One who does have it all figured out!

CHAPTER 3

Everything Depends on Me

"Mom, are you okay?" my son sheepishly asked me.

No, I really wasn't. Feeling outmatched and overwhelmed, I burst into tears. It had been one of those days when the kids seemed to be bickering continuously, the house looked like the site of a natural disaster, and I had been up most of the night battling another one of Bella's asthma attacks. When I have what seems like a thousand emails in my inbox, projects looming, laundry piling up, bills to be paid, and meals to plan, it can feel like the weight of the world is on my shoulders. I can't help but think, "Everything depends on me!"

Yes, sometimes it feels like the full weight of Schwenk Family, Incorporated, rests on my shoulders. If I don't plan dinner, I can't just find a quick bite to eat. I have a whole family to feed. If I go away for one day it takes me at least two to catch up. If I ignore the laundry for a few days, it seems like every piece of clothing in my house needs to be laundered. If I don't pick up constantly to reduce the clutter, I soon face a mountain of mayhem in every room of my home. There is a ton we moms are responsible for!

Sometimes—well, most of the time—it feels like I am trapped in one of those revolving doors at the entrance of a fancy hotel. Except my life is anything but fancy. The door doesn't lead into a beautiful hotel lobby. I just keep spinning around and around, faster and faster, from laundry room to kitchen to car!

The stress of everyday life as a mom is real. Our responsibilities are many and the consequences of our attentiveness—or lack thereof—are significant. The load can weigh heavy on a momma's heart. It can leave us wondering if we can do it—and do it well. It can also leave us feeling like everything depends on us.

KEEPING IT ALL UNDER CONTROL

When we start to feel like everything depends on us, we may give up and check out. We let the house go to shambles while we shop at the mall or update Facebook, or we offload too many of our parenting duties onto babysitters or husbands.

What's more likely, though, is that we try to do it all and keep everything under control. We get used to everything being under our watchful eyes, and we don't want to let our children out of our sight—literally. For example, I remember when we were in the final stages of making decisions about a house we were moving into and had to choose how many windows we wanted in our bedroom. It already had three windows facing the front yard. The question was whether to add one more window, facing our neighbor's house, that would allow us to see a good portion of our backyard.

"I think we should add the window," I said to my husband.

"Why?" he asked.

"So I can see the kids playing in the side yard if I am upstairs," I said.

Patrick didn't quite agree. Back and forth we went, until he finally convinced me that I was not having a window problem, I was having a control problem. Ouch! Point taken. I wanted to be able to see every move my children made, keeping an ever-protective eye on my flock.

For a protective momma, letting go of control is not easy, but holding onto control is exhausting! It's easy to maintain control when our kids are young. They need us for everything and we have a lot of control over them. We decide what they will eat, when they will eat, what clothes they'll wear, when they will nap, how much TV and which shows they can watch, and when they will go to bed. This is appropriate. But as they get older, spend more time away from us, and engage more with the world, it becomes appropriate to loosen some of that control.

Of course we still need to set boundaries, protect our kids, help influence their choices, or even say no to our kid's desires that are dangerous or unbiblical. But it is not our responsibility to control or change their personalities, their every activity, their choice of friends, or their dreams and goals. Nor can we (ultimately) control their spiritual choices through lists of rules or keeping them at home as much as possible. If we believe deep inside that everything depends on us, we will continue to grasp for control at every turn. Being over-controlling is one of the surest symptoms of a self-reliant, everything-depends-on-me mom.

The good news is that everything *doesn't* depend on us. We are not momming alone. While we might feel that way at times,

> *Where we are weak, God is strong. Where we fall short, God is faithful.*

we serve a God who is far more powerful, wise, and loving than we ever could be. And he is with us, reigning and ruling over all things (Ephesians 1:22) and parenting our children in countless ways we cannot see. He is at work in us and through us. Where we are weak, God is strong. Where we fall short, God is faithful.

Growing to be a better mom is not about gaining control so we can hold everything together and make everything work. It is about growing more dependent on our wise, good, and powerful Father. It is about giving up control and learning to surrender to God instead of trying to be God. The apostle Paul himself had to learn this important lesson.

GROWING MORE DEPENDENT

At one point Paul wrote to a church in Corinth about all the struggles he had faced in his ministry. You name it, he had been through it: jail, harassment, physical threats, poverty, and more (see 2 Corinthians 11:23–30). He sums up everything he went through: "We were under great pressure, far beyond our ability to endure, so that we despaired of life itself. Indeed, we felt we had received the sentence of death." Then he concludes: "But this happened that we might not rely on ourselves but on God, who raises the dead" (2 Corinthians 1:8–9).

God was using all this suffering and pressure to teach Paul to rely on God's strength. When Paul felt like he was being squashed, God was actually teaching him a valuable lesson: everything doesn't depend on you. You don't have to carry this weight alone. I am at work. Lean on me. I'll give you what you need to accomplish this.

How's that for relief? Do you feel the weight lifted? Do you feel the freedom that comes from letting God be God? As important as momming is, the mission is not ours alone. We are important for sure, but this is God's work. So we need to rest in the grace he gives us and allow him to work his plans and purposes for our families.

We all need this reminder. Even the apostle Paul did. That is why Paul later was able to say, "But he said to me, 'My grace is sufficient for you, for my power is made perfect in weakness.' Therefore I will boast all the more gladly about my weaknesses, so that Christ's power may rest on me. That is why, for Christ's sake, I delight in weaknesses, in insults, in hardships, in persecutions, in difficulties. For when I am weak, then I am strong" (2 Corinthians 12:9–10).

The sooner we realize this, the sooner we begin to experience the blessing of our own weaknesses. God uses weakness to reveal his strength, to change us, to move us in a different direction, or to teach us something. Everything does *not* depend on us. Weakness wakes us up to this reality. We need to depend on God more and depend on ourselves less. It is our weaknesses that allow God's grace to strengthen us and help us mature. Growing into better moms is paradoxically not about gaining expertise but about giving up control and growing more dependent— something that often doesn't come naturally to moms!

So in which areas are you not trusting God right now? In which areas of momming are you trying to be God? What heavy load are you carrying that you need to give to your heavenly Father? He's waiting for you to come to him and surrender to him, so that you might enjoy the peace that comes from knowing he is in control of all things.

TRANSFORMING OUR WEAKNESSES

Recently, I received a scary text message from my husband. He had left early that morning for a follow-up appointment with his doctor, and I was expecting him back anytime. Then I got his text. He was on his way to the hospital in an ambulance!

That trip led to a day in the emergency room, followed by four days in the hospital. It was a scary week, as were the months after, while his doctor sought to determine exactly what was going on. It was a perfect setup for going into overdrive, attempting to become supermom and superwife who would keep it all together. I am glad I didn't choose to face it alone, as I might have done in the past. Instead, I turned to our church family. They were quick to do whatever they could to help us in our time of need. While it is always humbling to be on the receiving end, it is a blessing too. We witnessed them make meals, watch our kids, mow our grass, and faithfully pray for us. They were strengthening us in our weakness. We were learning it is okay to admit we need help.

Whether it comes in the form of a tragedy, a sudden illness, extra hours at work, difficult financial circumstances, a change in jobs, or a host of other things, marriage and family life is full of unexpected twists and turns. At some point, whether during a medical crisis or just a difficult day, everyone needs help. It might mean asking your church family for help, as I did. It might mean ceding an area of control to your husband. It might mean calling another mom for advice. Sometimes it means getting away for coffee with a friend. It's okay to ask for help because everything is not up to us. We weren't meant to carry the heavy load of momming alone. There is a reason God has placed people in our lives. We're meant for community. When we follow Jesus, we don't follow him alone.

When we feel like everything is up to us, momming is a lonely journey. We might quietly or secretly struggle to get by. One of the ways God works in us is through the people around us. Husbands, grandparents, friends, teachers, pastors, doctors, counselors, daycare workers, coaches, bosses, and even plumbers, painters, wait staff, and cleaning people—all of them have important roles in our mothering journeys. In some cases they help us to be better moms, but in many cases they actually help us do the challenging work of caring for our homes and raising our children!

Preschool children often have a lesson that teaches about "community helpers." They learn about police and firefighters, doctors and teachers, postal workers and garbage collectors. Perhaps we need to take a refresher course of our own, and relearn how many people are out there waiting to help—from the lactation consultant, to the children's librarian, to the soccer coach and the daycare worker.

When we choose to walk alone, we miss out on the countless ways God wants to work through his people, for his people. All of us are in this together. We shouldn't be surprised at our weaknesses, because we were never supposed to do everything ourselves or be the be-all and end-all for our children. Indeed, God asks only that we do our part, and with gratitude allow others to do their part too (see 1 Corinthians 12). Our feelings of weakness might be new to us, but they are not new to God. He knows our limitations; he knows we are dust (Psalm 103:14). He shows us our weaknesses so that we might turn to him and find mercy and grace in our times of need. God graciously exposes our hearts so we might be able to see who we really are, that we might become who he wants us to be. He doesn't wait for us to get strong, secure, confident, or healthy. He does his greatest work in and through our weaknesses.

We are not alone. Using the body of Christ, the people he has placed around us, God is able to do far more than we could ever imagine. Everything does not depend on us. As Paul points out, "The body is not made up of one part but of many" (1 Corinthians 12:14). Or in other words, "The momming is not done by one person but by many." God has put people in our lives to help us feed, clothe, nurse, support, coach, teach, entertain, encourage, discipline, protect, and love our children. Not only that, but God's power gives us the strength we need for whatever momming challenges come our way, and the humility we need to ask for and accept help. We can leave discouragement and fear behind. We can have hope. And we can depend on this: God "is able to do immeasurably more than all we ask or imagine, according to his power that is at work within us" (Ephesians 3:20).

CHAPTER 4

I Want the Perfect Home

When I heard my husband's voice, I knew immediately that something was wrong—not terribly wrong, like one of the kids was missing, but close. He was upstairs and I was downstairs. But I heard his voice and received his message of concern loud and clear!

We had just moved into a brand-new home, which was unlike any other home we had owned. Prior to this move, we had lived in old homes—homes that were seventy, eighty, to a hundred years old. I loved those homes, but with the charm came lots of imperfection and plenty of maintenance. So moving into a new home was amazing!

Everything looked beautiful. There were no dings in the walls. No scratches on the floors. No cracked sidewalks or oil spots on the driveway. Even the carpet was spotless and still smelled new. Everything was, well, perfect.

And then we moved in. We hadn't lived in our new home for one day when I heard my husband's voice from upstairs. I ran up the stairs yelling, "What? What?!" I was relieved to discover that all the kids were alive. The house was not on fire. The hamster was in its cage. My husband was okay. But I was not so relieved when I saw the hole in the wall of our daughters' bedroom!

Everyone was innocent of course. No one could quite account for how the gaping hole got there. But with some investigative work we determined that a piece of wood from our daughters' bunk bed had fallen against the wall—thus the large hole in the newly painted room of our brand new house. There's nothing like a hole in the wall to remind us that a house is meant to be lived in, not just looked at.

Whether we live in a new home or old home, it's easy for us as moms to get sucked into chasing after our image of the perfect home. We see the pictures on Instagram, Pinterest, or in *Better Homes and Gardens*. But I have a suspicion that no one lives in those homes. Or, at the least, the home is staged momentarily and then torn apart a few minutes after the picture is snapped!

In the real world, our homes are where life happens. They are the primary place we do the life-changing and life-shaping work of momming. We wrestle with our kids. Read books. Cook meals. Eat together. We do homework and talk about God. We invite friends, family, and neighbors in. Our home is supposed to be a place of joy and laughter, learning and loving.

Right now, as I am writing this, I can see footprints in our newly mulched landscaping beds from where our kids have fetched stray Nerf bullets. Our son's friend just rollerbladed across the front yard. I can see dust on the windowsill and in the corners of the wood floor. But this is home, and in a little bit we'll sit around the table. Talk about our day. Prepare and plan for a weekend together. Ignore the laundry. Let the grass grow another day, or two. Do our family devotions. Then we'll call it a night.

As appealing as the picture-perfect home is, our homes are where we live, not where we sightsee. It's the life we bring to a home that matters most. Home is not just where we share life, it is where we begin to give life to our kids. And not only our kids, but anyone who enters our homes.

HOW WE LIVE IN OUR HOMES MATTERS

Not long ago a young woman told us how much our family has meant to her. When she was a high school student, she spent a lot of time hanging out with us in our home. So much so that she became a part of our family! It wasn't uncommon for her to stop by for dinner, play with our kids, then hang out and stay up late, talking. Now, more than a decade later, she is a mom. She and her husband are serving in ministry, raising their own family, and cultivating a life together.

Recently, as we were talking about what had shaped her the most as she was growing up, she said something I didn't expect to hear but that I will always remember. The most influential, life-shaping experience for her wasn't the church services or messages. It wasn't a youth retreat or a worship experience. It was our home! She said, "I never knew what a family was supposed to look like until I came to your house."

Now don't get me wrong, we are far from the perfect family! But in God's timing and in God's way, our home provided an opportunity for her to see how a couple committed to serving Christ treated each other in marriage. She was able to witness the relationship between parents and children in a family that is doing its best to honor God. Our home—complete with dinged and scratched woodwork, baby dolls and trucks scattered across the floor, and a sometimes-frazzled mom trying to hold it all together—was a window into a whole new world that she desperately needed and wanted. A world that was very different from the one she grew up in. Our home helped to give her a life she had never known.

Wow! If ever I received a reality check on the importance of my role as a mom in God's plan for my family, it was then. Our homes have powerful potential for giving life to those around us. As God works in us, cultivating in us the heart of Jesus, we are able to cultivate a better home culture. This is important because our homes don't just define where we live; in many ways, our homes define who we will become.

Home is the first and main context for our kids to know and experience the love we have for them. Home is the space where we begin the lifelong process of teaching, training, and maturing. So how we live in our homes matters. What a joy and honor it is that we get to give our kids the first taste of who God is. As we love, give, serve, teach, and train, we are helping our kids begin to understand how God parents each of us. Our homes are to be filled with God's presence as we live for God's purposes. More than a beautiful or perfect-looking home, God desires our homes to be sacred spaces.

OUR HOME AS A "LITTLE TEMPLE"

In Jesus's day, the temple in Jerusalem was a sacred space, the place where God's presence dwelled. The Jewish people went to the temple to offer sacrifices, pray, worship God, and celebrate special feasts. The temple was to be like stepping into a piece of heaven on earth. Then something tragic happened. The temple was destroyed in AD 70.

Now what? Would God build a new temple? Where would they worship, celebrate, and enjoy the presence of God?

There would be many and varied answers to those questions. But one answer and solution was the Jewish home. In fact, many of the Jewish leaders began to refer to the home as a *miqdash me'at* (a small or little temple). Instead of God's presence dwelling in the temple in Jerusalem, each home would be a sacred space like a little temple. A greater emphasis would be placed on the Jewish home and family as a vehicle for passing on faith, teaching truth, and worshiping God together.

I've always loved this picture because it reminds me, as a mom, of how safe and sacred our home—our little temple— should be. Our home should be a place where our kids experience God's love. A place where we work to create and protect an atmosphere of belonging and security. A place where we teach and model God's truth.

The New Testament uses similar language to describe who we are in Christ. We are like temples, filled by the Holy Spirit (1 Corinthians 6:19–20). As God transforms us from the inside out to be sacred spaces, we in turn transform our homes to be sacred spaces through which God works in us and through us to shape our kids for eternity. But in order to cultivate our homes as sacred spaces, we need a solid foundation.

About ten years ago, we often drove by a hotel that looked like it was half built. For the longest time we couldn't figure out why it was taking so long for the building to be completed. Each time we drove by, the building stood very much like it had the last time we saw it.

Eventually, friends who lived in the area told us the story behind the unfinished hotel.

Apparently, the builders were nearly halfway finished when they discovered that the foundation was failing! They would have to tear the entire building down and start over with a new foundation. The mistake cost the builder hundreds of thousands of dollars, and probably someone's job.

Where we build and how we start is incredibly important. If we don't have the right foundation, our homes will eventually crumble. This was Jesus's point in a story he told about two builders. They each built a house, and both houses endured the same weather. But only one lasted. Notice what Jesus said in Matthew 7:24–27:

> Therefore everyone who hears these words of mine and puts them into practice is like a wise man who built his house on the rock. The rain came down, the streams rose, and the winds blew and beat against that house; yet it did not fall, because it had its foundation on the rock. But everyone who hears these words of mine and does not put them into practice is like a foolish man who built his house on sand. The rain came down, the streams rose, and the winds blew and beat against that house, and it fell with a great crash.

Only one house was built on the right foundation. Jesus used this story to remind us that we too need to build our life on the "rock," that is, Jesus himself. We are not only to hear his words, but to obey them. We should live for God's approval alone. As moms, we sometimes build on the wrong foundation by chasing other people's approval. We take pride in a seemingly picture-perfect home and family. We look to our kids' successes to give us our worth and well-being. Or we look to our career or accomplishments outside the home to fuel who we are. Our choice of foundations makes a difference.

But our worth is found in God's love for us, no matter what. This is the foundation that lasts. This is true in our hearts and in our homes.

PASSING ON WHAT WE POSSESS

As we begin to grow up in Christ, we will experience more of God's truth and grace in our lives. We will possess more and more of the abundant life he wants for us and will increasingly bear the fruit of love, joy, peace, patience, kindness, goodness, faithfulness, and self-control. The good news is, those around us will too!

When God changes our hearts, he also changes our homes. It has always been God's desire for parents to pass on the faith they possess in their own hearts. We see this in the Old Testament when Moses gave God's instructions to the Israelites. God commanded them to be sure to pass on their faith to the next generation. Much of this work would happen in and through the home. "Love the LORD your God with all your heart and with all your soul and with all your strength. These commandments that I give you today are to be on your hearts. Impress them on your children. Talk about them when you sit at home and when you walk along the road, when you lie down and when you get up" (Deuteronomy 6:5–7).

What a privilege we have as moms to participate in the life transformation of our children! God's truth is to be at the center—the foundation—of every parent's life as they pass on faith to their children. They are even commanded to write God's Word on the doorframes of their homes (Deuteronomy 6:9).

The Jewish people, then and now, took this seriously. If you enter a Jewish home today, you might notice a small wooden or metal box attached to the right doorframe at the entrance of the house. Inside is a *mezuzah* scroll, a rolled piece of paper or parchment with Deuteronomy 6:4–9 and Deuteronomy 11:13–21 written in Hebrew. It serves as a reminder to parents that they are to use their home to help pass their faith on to their children, faithfully instructing them in God's Word and God's ways.

Home is a place where God's presence is felt and his purposes followed.

As moms, we are not just trying to raise good kids. By God's grace we are working to raise followers of Jesus. We don't have to be Bible scholars or pastors to do this. God calls parents—moms and dads—to do this! In our house, one of my privileges as a mom is to help make family devotions a priority. While we do not do this perfectly, or always consistently, we make time as a family to read the Bible. We discuss the stories and ask questions about what each child learned or had trouble understanding. We also memorize Scripture, making it fun by offering different rewards.

Raising followers of Jesus is about more than me just reading the Bible. It is about making its teachings a part of everyday life. Talking about and acting upon my beliefs is critical to passing on my faith. On a recent trip to the store with one of our teenage children, I started talking about inviting some of our neighbors over for dinner and praying for God to give our family opportunities to meet new people.

As we talked, I commented that we are never too young to be used by God to reach other people. Before I knew it, our daughter had pulled out her phone and texted a friend in the neighborhood to invite her to youth group! The classroom of life provides everyday opportunities to talk about and live out our faith.

Jesus is the "rock" of our hearts so that he can also be the rock—or foundation—of our homes. There is plenty of pressure to be the perfect mom and to have the picture-perfect home. It's easy to lose sight of the foundation we are supposed to be building on. The home is not just to be a place that looks good or is admired; the home is a place to be lived in for God's purposes. Our homes are shaping our kids' hearts. And so, in a very real way, they will always take a piece of our home with them.

HOME IS WHERE THE HEART IS

It's an old saying. I had heard it hundreds of times before, and you probably have too. But when I saw it recently at a local restaurant, it was as if I was seeing it for the first time. A simple wooden sign proclaimed in large whitewashed letters: Home is where the heart is.

What struck me that day was that home is not just a place my heart is fond of; home is a place that forms our hearts. Home is where our children's hearts begin to be formed by moms and dads. Of course, our children's hearts will be shaped, for better or for worse, in countless ways and places. But the home is the first and often most profound formative place.

Home is a refuge or shelter from all that is going on "outside." We make it a home by filling it with our presence and God's presence. It is a place marked off for meaningful relationships, unconditional love, intentional guidance, and uninhibited joy. As moms, we have the privilege of building that kind of home for our families.

So what kind of home are you building? Is it your dream home? Is it your castle? Or is it a "little temple," a place carved out from the rest of the world?

I can't help but wonder what our kids will remember about home. I pray they will remember our home as somewhere special and sacred—a place where mom and dad weren't always perfect, but Jesus was at the center. A place where God's presence was felt and his purposes followed. A place that's not just where they used to live, but a place they always take with them in their hearts.

In short: the perfect home.

CHAPTER 5

Who Am I, Anyway?

oney, you have to try this product we are selling!" I proclaimed to my husband. "It says it helps with hair loss."

He was noticeably skeptical but also undoubtedly interested. "Okay, I'll try it," he said.

That was so easy, I thought to myself. *I love doing this!*

Almost a year later, Patrick was still bald, but I still loved my job. That was one of the reasons it was so difficult for me to think about giving it up. I love people and I love sales. Give me a product I believe in and I can get anyone excited about it—even my husband! That's why I loved working in retail, and this job was even more fun than that. I discovered new gifts and abilities I never knew I had. I loved—I mean really loved—leading teams, casting vision, and developing new trainees. Plus, I enjoyed the fun of selling a product I thought was amazing! But that wasn't all I loved about the job.

I didn't realize it at the time, but my job gave me a sense of worth and identity. Before the job I was "just a mom," a myth I had let my heart believe. I originally went back to work in order to bring in some additional income, but the job gave me so much more. I was good at it, and people knew it. After several years I had become a competent leader, successful marketer, and an influencer—and I was contributing financially to our family. I felt a sense of importance—even pride—in my job, that I didn't feel as a mom.

But even while having a job I enjoyed and excelled at, I began to wonder if there might be something different for me. I began to wrestle with whether or not this was the right job—the right place to use my gifts. Was this really how I wanted to be known? I had a heart for ministry and a love for others. I felt torn between where God was leading me and where I was.

These are legitimate questions to ask. Each of us needs to be intentional about what we are doing, who we are becoming, and where God is leading. But there was something more unsettling about my struggle at that time. My work had become my worth. More than anything else, I was wrestling with whether or not giving up my job would also be giving up a part of me.

FINDING OUR TRUE SOURCE OF WORTH

Who am I? is one of the most basic questions we ask ourselves. When we ask that question, we're asking a question not only of identity, but also of worth. And you would think that becoming a mother would be the ultimate answer: I am the mother of this beautiful child! After all, what closer relationship is there? What more worthy calling could there be?

Yet paradoxically, becoming a mother can also launch a new search for worth and meaning. We may realize or sense that momming doesn't fulfill every aspect of who we are—we have education, training, talents, and interests that go beyond our role as mothers. So we may turn to jobs, volunteer work, or hobbies to help us express our identities and give us a sense of worth and value.

In my case, I had let what I was doing—my job—define who I was. What I was doing gave me a positive sense of self-worth. But often what we're doing, or what we feel we aren't doing, can have the opposite effect and degrades our sense of worth. Regardless of the positive or negative impact, we are all susceptible to having a misplaced source of value or worth. Psychologist Joanna Collicutt says, "It could be argued that our readiness to doubt our own worth is a defining aspect of fallen human nature."[1] Everyone wrestles with the questions of "Who am I? Am I good enough?" We are all searching for a sense of value.

So the real question is not *if* we are looking but *where* we are looking. If we are going to allow God to transform us from the inside out, we have to make sure we are placing our worth as moms in the right place. Or, as we'll see, in the right person. I was looking to my job to provide greater feelings of worth, significance, and joy. But my longing was misplaced. It was dangerous to my own heart and stood in the way of me becoming who God wanted me to be. And there are many ways we can misplace our source of worth.

We may look to our accomplishments to define us. This is where I struggled. I allowed my successes to provide my sense of well-being. Some misplaced sources of worth might be our workplaces or our talents and abilities that help us feel productive and valuable. Or if our marriage is healthy and our kids are doing well, we may feel a sense of pride—look at what a great mom I am!—as if we have done it all ourselves. Even our walk with Christ, when it is going smoothly, may be a source of significance and worth. If we're not careful, our spiritual "success" may become a place of pride, judgment, or self-righteousness! "I am my success" is a dangerous source of significance.

Not only might we let our accomplishments define who we are, sometimes we let our failures do the same. A job loss or demotion can leave us feeling less than who we really are. Sometimes we even allow our kids' choices to define who we are. We believe we are a failure as a mom if a son or daughter has walked away from the faith or is going through a difficult season. If we're not careful, our self-worth can be influenced by the ways we (or those close to us) have messed up, fallen short, or flat out gotten it wrong!

The greatest treasure . . . is the truth that we are loved by God.

Some moms who were physically, verbally, or sexually abused as children have come to see their worth not in terms of their successes or failures, but in terms of what has been done to them. My heart breaks for moms who feel shamed and unloved for years, if not for decades. They were not the ones who sinned, but someone sinned against them. In other cases, smaller or less noticeable influences may affect our view of ourselves in a negative way. Maybe we didn't receive the love and care we needed from a parent. Maybe hurtful words and actions were directed toward us when we were teenagers or young adults. Whether such sins committed against us were big or small, they can lead us to see ourselves as less than we are.

Another misplaced source of worth may be our "stuff." Some of us see ourselves as being valuable because of what belongs to us. Our material possessions—a house, neighborhood, clothing, and more—may give us the feeling of "enough." The Bible warns us about this in 1 John 2:16: "Everything in the world—the lust of the flesh, the lust of the eyes, and the pride of life—comes not from the Father but from the world."

Some of us look to family or friends to provide a sense of worth. We might take pride in our family of origin because it is well known or respected in the community. Perhaps we feel a sense of significance because of who our friends are. We enjoy knowing and being known by certain people. We name-drop or associate with certain people because of who they are. We may let our proximity to people who we think are important give us feelings of importance.

Not one of these ways we try to find our worth will satisfy us or lead to the lives God wants for us. Instead, they leave us always trying to measure up so that we can feel like we are "enough." These pursuits are like moving targets, pulling us in every direction. They create in our hearts a sense of restlessness, discontent, and unhappiness that can lead to feelings of anger, bitterness, envy, insecurity, or fear.

Our hearts need a place to rest. When we are not sure of who we are or where our worth comes from, our hearts can feel insecure, unsettled, easily swayed, and discontent. There is a peace, joy, and freedom that fills and fuels our hearts when our worth is anchored in the right place. And when we think we've lost our identity and value, the real source of our worth might be closer than we think.

A TREASURE WE CANNOT LOSE

All wedding rings are special, but mine was especially valuable to me because of the people who had it before me. It originally belonged to my grandmother, then my mom, then me. It wasn't just a ring; it was a treasure. And that is why I went into panic mode when it went missing.

We had gone south to find warmer weather in February. Each day, before we went to the beach, I would take off my ring and place it next to our bed or next to the hand soap by the sink. One afternoon, after returning from a full day at the beach, I went to slip on my ring only to discover it was gone! It was nowhere to be found. It wasn't by our bed. It wasn't by the sink. And it certainly wasn't on my finger.

"Honey!" I yelled for my husband. "Have you seen my ring?" I knew he probably hadn't, but I was quickly running out of options. "I think I lost my wedding ring. I know it was here when we left. Please, Lord, help me find it!"

The last two days of vacation were far from a vacation for me. I searched and searched, turning over in my head what I could have done with the ring. I had all sorts of ideas as to how it might have disappeared. By the time we headed home, I was sure one of the maids had stolen it.

Our vacation was over, but I could not let go of the ring I had misplaced. I would think about it, mentally retracing my steps. I even called the hotel to see if by chance someone had turned it in. Nothing. My ring was gone.

Nearly a year later I heard a *ping* by my feet as I was going through some old clothes in my daughter's closet. Something hit the wood floor by my feet, and when I bent down to see what had made the noise, I discovered my wedding ring! I stood there staring at it in disbelief for a few moments before I began yelling, "Honey! I found my ring, my *wedding* ring!" The wedding ring I had been looking for was not lost. No one had stolen it. It must have gotten mixed in with our clothing on that vacation, made its way home with us, and stayed tucked into my daughter's clothes as I put them away in the closet. The treasure I had been looking for had been right in front of me all along.

I didn't need to go out and find the ring or buy a new one. It was a treasure I had to discover—rediscover—much like the greatest truth that can be said of us. The greatest treasure—that no one can take away from us—is the truth that we are loved by God. God is the true source of our worth. What he says about us matters most.

A TREASURE GIVEN, NOT EARNED

Our real source of worth is not found in our successes, our possessions, or even our children. Our worth is found in what our Father says about us (1 John 3:1). If we are in Christ, we are fully and completely loved. By faith, all that is true of Jesus is true of us. We are accepted. Secure. Spotless. Clean. Free. Worthy beyond what we can even imagine.

We are God's "beloved." We can't make God love us more and we can't make God love us less. We are his daughters, daughters he delights in. Henri Nouwen once wrote that "self-rejection is the greatest enemy of the spiritual life because it contradicts the sacred voice that calls us the 'Beloved.' Being the Beloved expresses the core truth of our existence."[2]

Did you hear that? We have a Father who speaks over us. His

voice is the voice of our Creator and Savior. His voice is louder than all the other voices we often hear—voices that tell us we aren't loved, aren't "good enough," or don't measure up. When our kids don't obey, we still have a Father who loves us. When the house is a mess and dinner isn't ready, we still have a Father who is pleased with us. There is a joy and peace available to us when our kids don't get into the school we wanted. When we are at home with a sick child and nothing we had planned gets accomplished, God still loves us. And even in those rare seasons when everything is going great, knowing and being known by God is even greater.

No matter what other voices say or how loudly they say it, our Father's approval and assessment of worth is enough. He is pleased with us because of what Christ has done for us. We are of immeasurable worth to the one who matters most. It is his love for us in Christ that defines us, protects us, and cultivates good hearts within us.

Perhaps no greater statement of worth is found in the life of Jesus than at his baptism. He is getting ready to start his public ministry. Long before he does anything of real significance in the world, before any miracle or triumph, he receives what matters most—his Father's approval. Jesus was the "Beloved" of the Father: "As soon as Jesus was baptized, he went up out of the water. At that moment heaven was opened, and he saw the Spirit of God descending like a dove and alighting on him. And a voice from heaven said, 'This is my Son, whom I love; with him I am well pleased'" (Matthew 3:16–17).

God the Father wanted everyone to know that Jesus had his approval. His hand of favor was upon him. The beautiful thing about the good news of Jesus is that when we come to faith in him, all that is his becomes ours. We are "in him." God's approval of Jesus is ours. God's acceptance of Jesus is ours. When the Father speaks over Jesus, he speaks over us: "This is my daughter, whom I love; with her I am well pleased."

We don't have to earn our worth or work to keep it. We only have to receive God's love and learn to rest in it. Like my wedding ring, our ultimate identity and worth only needs to be discovered, or for some, rediscovered. It is freely given.

We are loved, so we can give up searching for a sense of worth. We can stop asking, "Who am I?" It's not about whether we have a good job, whether we are the "perfect" mom, whether we have the right "stuff," or whether we know the right people. In Christ, we find the most valuable treasure of all. We are loved. It is enough to be known by God, loved, and accepted by him. The only thing left to seek is who we are becoming as we grow to be more like him.

So next time you ask yourself, "Who am I?" answer, "I am the daughter of my heavenly Father."

He gives us our identity. *He* bestows our worth. His view of us is the lost treasure we need to search for, find, and reclaim.

CHAPTER 6

I Miss My Friends!

A t the time, we thought it was a great idea," she told me. "We were all friends and most of us had young kids, so we thought going on vacation together would be fun."

"So what happened?" I asked. I had no idea where she was going with this story.

"It was a disaster! That's what happened!" She continued, "One couple, without kids, always wanted to go out. Our friends with a two-year-old spent every waking minute trying to keep their child out of the lake, away from the stairs, and nowhere near the fire pit! Another couple didn't want to do anything that would disrupt their son's eating and sleeping schedule."

She sounded exasperated. "So we ended up coming home early. I'll never go away with friends again!" she proclaimed. Then she softened and asked me, "How do you do this mom thing and still be a good friend?"

That I understood! It's tough to be a good mom and a good friend. Even for moms who have great friends, momming changes things. Momming has a way of creating distance from even some of our closest friends.

When we begin having kids, our friends are likely having kids too. Even if we are able to maintain those friendships, change is inevitable. We can't have friends over for dinner and stay up late talking or watching a movie like we used to. Meeting a friend for coffee is no longer as easy as running out the door to the coffee shop. Now we have to think about snacks to take, a change of clothes, extra diapers, and something to keep our kids entertained while we're attempting adult conversation.

Getting together when kids are involved takes a lot of work. Between everyday busyness, sickness, and naps, even connecting at the park feels like trying to run a marathon! And even when you do manage to get together with another mom on a play date, the constant interruptions and noise from our children make it difficult to connect deeply. No wonder many moms, even those who have had good friends, feel like meaningful friendships are almost impossible during this season of life.

As a young mom, I couldn't understand why I felt so isolated, disconnected, and alone. I had a good marriage. I loved being a mom to several healthy and happy kids. Yet there was a longing in my heart for friendship, for meaningful connection I was missing. Perhaps Facebook, Instagram, Twitter, or other social media would have helped—a little—but those didn't exist when I first became a mom. Besides, social networks can increase our depression and increase our paranoia that we don't measure up or are missing out. And even with our ever-present cell phones and internet connectedness, nearly every mom struggles with feeling disconnected. We are starving for real, meaningful, face-to-face friendships.

Many of us feel a great void in our relationships. But friends matter because they help encourage us when we feel like nothing is going right. And friends who know us well enough to challenge us are a gift, not only for our momming, but also for the refining of our own souls. Friendships don't just help us survive the momming years; friendships are instrumental in shaping who we are, and even more important, who God wants us to become. This is why the Bible has so much to say about friends, and especially, choosing the right friends.

CHOOSING FRIENDS

Our daughter Bella was invited to an all-day birthday party with a friend. It was a fun-filled time of painting, pizza, cake, and of course lots of squealing, giggling girls! When she came home, we noticed she was not acting like herself. She was using unusual expressions, had a different attitude, and even responded to instruction in ways that clearly were not the norm. I wanted to ask, "Who are you and where is my daughter?" However, wisdom told me to keep quiet.

Then it clicked: she was acting like some of the girls she had just been with. It took only about six hours with friends (not long, but long enough!) to begin shaping and reshaping certain behaviors.

We are quick to spot when a child's friends are not good for them, but how often do we notice that in our own friendships? To state the obvious: not everyone is a suitable friend. The best friendships, the friendships that help us grow as mothers and believers, happen when we choose our friends carefully. God wants us to choose our friends wisely because our communities of relationships profoundly shape our character. Notice a few highlights from the book of Proverbs:

- "Walk with the wise and become wise, for a companion of fools suffers harm" (Proverbs 13:20).
- "The righteous choose their friends carefully, but the way of the wicked leads them astray" (Proverbs 12:26).
- "One who has unreliable friends soon comes to ruin, but there is a friend who sticks closer than a brother" (Proverbs 18:24).

We are told to "walk with the wise" because when we do, we have the opportunity to "become wise." But the opposite is true too. The companion of "fools" rubs off on us as well. God reminds us that the righteous choose their friends carefully, with much thought and prayer.

Aren't these the kind of friendships we long for? When we choose our friends wisely, we stick together. The word *stick* is the same word used of Adam and Eve when they became one flesh. The Bible describes them as being united, stuck together like glue ("cleave" in some translations of Genesis 2:24). True friendship creates an intimate bond. Friends stick close—close like glue. Friends shape who we are becoming. So we need to choose them wisely.

I have found this to be true in my own life. It was a friend who first invited me to church. It was friends who spoke into my life when I was a new Christian. It was a friend who, early in our marriage, significantly shaped how I understood God's calling for me as a wife and mom. It was friends who walked beside me and helped me to mourn and process my miscarriages. Today I have friends who pray for me, encourage me, and challenge me to keep pressing on and pursuing Christ every step of the way, and I do the same for them.

I'll never forget the friend who dropped everything to stay with the rest of our kids as we frantically rushed our son Noah to the emergency room. I'll always remember the night a small group of moms huddled together in our family room, praying for God to soften the heart of the son of one of the moms, who had walked away from Christ. Then there were the months I steadfastly prayed with a friend for her husband to return, showering her with Scriptures to keep her strong along the way. I love friends who make time to grab coffee and friends who watch my kids so I can run to the store. In so many different ways, I have experienced the blessing of good friendships.

As I look back, I see God has blessed me with tremendous friends at critical times in my life. These friendships changed as I went through different seasons. Many of these friends were women I sought out through church or a Bible study. But God graciously provided not just friends, but the right friends. These friendships didn't just happen. They took time. And they took commitment.

KEEPING FRIENDSHIPS REAL

Like many young children, I had an imaginary friend. I was an only child with a vivid imagination, so my "friend" and I did everything together. We dressed up dolls, played school, and talked about life. We went to the store, the park, and everywhere else I wanted to go. And my "friend" and I always got along. Ours was the perfect relationship—because it was imaginary!

It wasn't real life.

Fortunately, I grew out of that phase. But the truth is, even moms are known to create imaginary friends. Friends who always remember our birthdays. Friends who seem to know exactly when we need an encouraging text. Friends who are always there to watch our kids when we need them. Friends who are funny, empathetic, generous, selfless, and pretty much like Jesus except for the minor detail that they aren't real!

Our perfect, imaginary friends don't exist. Instead, we get real friends. As great as they are, they are friends who, like us, are still works in progress. They love but not perfectly. They care but are not always there for us. They listen but don't always understand. They can't be just like Jesus because they're human.

As important as friendships are, we need to remember that there are no perfect friends. Friendships are good, but they are not a replacement for God. So we need to keep the right perspective and have appropriate expectations for our friendships. Even our best, most intimate, and most reliable friendships need a reality check. We need to remember that we live in the real world, not a world of imaginary and perfect friends. And how do we do that? The New Testament tells us to make room for one another and to give each other space to grow. This is how Paul says it, "Always be humble and gentle. Be patient with each other, making allowance for each other's faults because of your love" (Ephesians 4:2 NLT). We are to be humble and gentle, recognizing that not one of us *is* a perfect friend and not one of us *has* a perfect friend.

True friendship is grounded in true love. In his book *A Grief Observed*, C. S. Lewis describes the miracle of this love as "the power of seeing through its own enchantments and yet not being disenchanted."[3] True love knows that people and friendships

> *We are to be humble and gentle, recognizing that not one of us is a perfect friend and not one of us has a perfect friend.*

aren't perfect. True love looks through the fantasy of imaginary friendship to see what is real. A friendship built on reality has full knowledge of the other person—the faults, shortcomings, and weaknesses—and still chooses to love. What a beautiful picture of the kind of friendships we need during these challenging years of momming.

Friendships that are real and grounded in true love are the kind of friendships that provide a safe, caring, and nurturing environment where we can be who we really are. Once I was having breakfast at a local cafe with a good friend when she broke down and cried. She had been bottling up the stress of the battle she was having with her youngest and couldn't hold it in any longer. She didn't need me to fix the problem; she needed a safe place. A person she knew she didn't have to pretend for. She needed to be honest and admit how much she was hurting. She needed love more than she needed a lesson on how to parent.

True friendship during such challenges is a blessing. The right friends are godly and wise, supportive and encouraging. They help us not only to get through life's trials, but ultimately to grow closer to Christ. That's exactly what the best friendships do—spur us on toward a greater purpose than the friendship itself.

FRIENDSHIPS WITH A PURPOSE

Friendships often develop in different ways. Maybe we meet someone at a local farmer's market, book club, or park. We develop friends through our children's sports or activities. With some friends we go out for coffee. With other moms we walk in the neighborhood or grab lunch when we can. But the best friendships don't end there. As important as these friendships are, our friendships need to be built on something even bigger.

The Bible reminds us that the best friendships are the ones that draw us closer to Christ. Sometimes this means not only having fun together, but also allowing our friendships to challenge us. As much as we need encouragement and good times with friends, I'm grateful for the friends who not only love by encouraging me, but the ones who aren't afraid to say unpleasant things too.

This proverb illustrates this important quality of friendship well: "As iron sharpens iron, so one person sharpens another" (Proverbs 27:17). Another proverb wisely states: "Better is open rebuke than hidden love. Wounds from a friend can be trusted, but an enemy multiplies kisses" (Proverbs 27:5–6). "Hidden love," as Proverbs 27:5 says, is no love at all. When we don't tell our friends the truth, we are actually loving ourselves more. It's closer to being an enemy than a true friend!

I am blessed to have several friends who are always looking out for me. This doesn't mean they are always there to defend me or praise me for everything I am doing right. Rather, they are friends who share a vision for friendship that serves a greater purpose. They are friends I trust to care enough about me to keep an eye on who I am becoming and how I am representing Christ in my ministry and my life. They are true friends who are willing to take the risk of some friction between us because they love me and care about who I am becoming. I know they are always ready to warn me and hold me accountable if I seem to be straying, and they trust me enough to do the same for them.

Friendships built on purpose include relationships not only with friends who are like us, but also with those who are different from us. We see this kind of friendship in the disciples whom Jesus called into friendship with God and with one another: "Greater love has no one than this: to lay down one's life for one's friends. You are my friends if you do what I command. I no longer call you servants, because a servant does not know his master's business. Instead, I have called you friends, for everything that I learned from my Father I have made known to you" (John 15:13–15).

This was a group of friends who had the shared purpose of following Jesus, but they were also very different from one another. There are amazing possibilities when we are united around a similar purpose in Christ but are radically different from each other. For example, my friends vary in age and personality, but they have all been used by God to make me a better woman and mom. I remember when my friend Sally challenged me to empathize with my daughter; it dramatically transformed my relationship with my daughter for the better. My friend Karen always tells it like it is. She isn't afraid to lovingly and carefully point me in the right direction if I am feeling overwhelmed. My friend Sandra isn't afraid to ask how I am doing. She prays for me faithfully and gently points me back to what matters most in my life.

When Jesus called his disciples, he did more than recruit workers for a cause. And he was focusing on more than their relationships with one another. Jesus was constantly pointing them toward the heart of God. He was constantly encouraging them to engage in kingdom priorities and activities. Their friendships were not a feel-good social clique; they were life-changing relationships centered on knowing, loving, and serving God.

This is the mark of a true friendship: it is built on a greater purpose. As we are shaping our kids, God is using our friends to shape us. These friendships matter. They encourage us, support us, challenge us, and by God's grace, help us not just to be better moms, but to become more like Christ.

CHAPTER 7

I Have to Be on Top of My Game

Back when I was newly married and had one baby at home, I decided to do some decorating of our turn-of-the-century home. Built in 1903, the house was full of character but also greatly in need of some TLC. Still, I was young and ambitious and thought we needed to make the house our own. But that wasn't going to be easy.

We were barely getting by on my husband's salary as a pastor. Not only was home décor out of our budget, it was also out of my giftings! Sure, I had seen a few fixer-upper and makeover shows on HGTV—but just enough to be dangerous! So a friend who had the right connections offered to help. I couldn't wait to find out what she had learned when she had asked one of her designer friends for some advice.

A few days later we sat on the couch in our living room. "So what did she say?" I eagerly asked my friend.

"Well, first she asked me what your style was," she said,

beginning to laugh. "I told her you didn't really have a style because you were in ministry." And then she went on to tell me what her friend thought would "dress up" our home.

I truly can't remember how we decorated that room. My brain got stuck on "We didn't have a style because we were in ministry." I replayed her comment in my mind countless times trying to figure out what she meant. It was an innocent comment, and I doubt she meant any ill will. But that didn't change how I interpreted it or how much it hurt. The comment rattled around in my head and finally settled in my heart.

What I heard and felt in that short conversation was, "Your home needs work, your home isn't very cute, and the bottom line is, you really don't have it together in the style department and you never will." Ouch! I felt like I had failed. As a woman. As a wife. As a mom. And definitely as a homemaker.

I had read the articles and seen the pictures of other people's homes. I knew ours was a far cry from the ones in the magazines. I knew I had a long way to go, but my friend's comment left me feeling like a complete failure. So much for trying to make our home a haven. Not only was I not on top of my game, I apparently wasn't even in the game!

This happened years ago, long before Facebook, Pinterest, and Instagram. Now it seems the pressure to be on top of it all is even greater. Everywhere a mom looks she sees pictures of delicious foods, designer décor, creative crafts, stylish clothes, and the list goes on. Women in general, and moms in particular, have a lot to live up to!

We all know we face a lot of pressure to be on top of our game. And it's not just in some things, it's in everything! There is pressure to be great, beautiful, energetic, and accomplished. We feel pressure to have champion kids. Pressure to have a picture-perfect home. And, of course, pressure to have it all and make it look easy. Nothing is more dangerous to our hearts than the pressure of trying to live up to these unrealistic expectations.

We must stop comparing and competing if we want to experience the lives God has for us.

All the images of perfection create a standard that the average mom feels less than adequate to achieve. And the pressure to be on top of our game in everything can steal the abundant lives God has for us. Maybe it's time to lift the pressure and point out that perfection is not a prerequisite to being a better mom. We have time and space to grow in grace between perfection and the mess.

LIFT THAT PRESSURE!

My close friend and I had been trying for months to get together. Sick kids. Snow days. Busy schedules. It was not easy to connect. Finally, my friend, who was a new mom again, was able to come over for some much-needed "adult" time.

We talked about school, marriage, church, and a whole lot more. Our kids were busy playing when, without much warning, her baby alerted us to the need to eat—now! Feeling a bit flustered and frustrated that our time for conversation was ending so quickly, she asked where she might pacify her screaming child.

I showed her to a room that would be perfect, and private, for nursing. A bit later she emerged. The baby looked happy, the kind of happy when your belly is full. My friend looked happy too. But it was more than happy. She had a smile on her face she could barely conceal.

I was curious. "What's up?" I asked. "What is so funny?"

"I saw something in your room," she said.

Now really curious, I nervously fished for more. "Ummm . . . what!?" Her answer was nothing secretive or terribly important—at least not to me, but it was to her. She had seen the pile of laundry scattered across our bedroom floor. It looked similar to how a front yard looks when a pack of unruly raccoons tips over a trash can and hunts for sustenance!

I didn't understand why this was such a big deal until she explained, "I am sooo glad you have loads of laundry sitting around your house too. I thought it was just me! And I'm so glad you didn't care that I saw it!"

The pressure to be on top of her game had been lifted. Something as insignificant as dirty laundry took the pressure off this new mom to be perfect and on her game all the time. She didn't have to have it all together. And she was relieved to discover I didn't either.

I get this response from other moms too. Not long ago I posted a photo of our daughters' room. It looked like a tornado had barreled through. Clothes were everywhere. Stuffed animals. Shoes. Part of a hamster cage. There was a bed in there somewhere. Within minutes of posting this picture, the comments started streaming in:

"Amen!"

"Thanks for being real."

"This looks very, very familiar!"

"I have hope that my child will one day grow out of this. Sighhhh . . ."

"I am relieved I am not the only one."

All pressure, being lifted.

IN THE GAME INSTEAD OF ON TOP OF YOUR GAME

I want to share a wonderful truth with you. As moms, we don't always have to be on *top* of our game; God just calls us to be *in* the game.

The fear of what others think can be a powerful force that wages war on our hearts. For years, I silently lived under the weight of trying to convince others I was on top of my game—that I had it all together: capable, competent, in charge, under control. I wasn't trying to be a supermom. I just wanted others to think I was a good mom—a good mom who could at least decorate her home.

I put pressure on myself that I thought was from others' expectations. I was trying to live up to their approval. The Bible encourages us to please people, but warns against people-pleasing. Notice how destructive to our hearts the Bible says that living for other people's approval can be:

> This is what the LORD says:
> "Cursed is the one who trusts in man,
>> who draws strength from mere flesh
>> and whose heart turns away from the LORD.
> That person will be like a bush in the wastelands;
>> they will not see prosperity when it comes.

They will dwell in the parched places of the desert,
in a salt land where no one lives."

JEREMIAH 17:5–6

The mom who "draws strength," or attempts to, from other people's approval will be like a bush being blown around in the desert. This kind of heart is not secure, well anchored, or alive. It is being tossed around, battered, and cannot find a resting place.

But there's good news! The one who sets her heart on the Lord's approval is like a tree planted by streams of water. Sturdy. Well rooted. Drawing strength from living water. Alive and bearing much fruit (Jeremiah 17:7–8). Isn't that what we really want? Isn't that the game we want to be in?

Living life well and being a better mom isn't about fearing people. It is about "fearing" God by revering and pursuing his approval. To fear God is to live a life more motivated to honor him than to make other people happy. It is to see God as our true place of safety, security, and strength. It is to live with the awareness that God is not only more powerful than the people in our lives; it is his assessment of our momming that is most important. We don't need to compete or compare with others; we need to stay close to Jesus. We are not called to run someone else's race; we're called to run our own.

RUN *YOUR* RACE

I'm not much of a runner, but my husband is. I've watched so many races and seen runners out for their daily jogs too many times to count. Every single time I find myself wishing I could run with that kind of endurance. But that's not the kind of race I am built, or called, to run.

Yet I know there *is* a race for me to run: "Therefore, since we are surrounded by such a great cloud of witnesses, let us throw off everything that hinders and the sin that so easily entangles. And let us run with perseverance the race marked out for us" (Hebrews 12:1).

What this passage *doesn't* say is as important as what it says. It doesn't tell us to win the race. It doesn't tell us to run fast. It tells us to run in such a way that we *finish*. Finishing the race well, in God's eyes, is more important than winning the race. And running the right race—the race marked out for *us*—is most important.

We are not supposed to run our parents' race. We are not commanded to run our neighbor's race. And when it comes to momming, we are not running another mom's race. Each of us is called to persevere in running our unique race, so there is no comparison, no competing. When we feel the pressure to be on top of it all, we need to remember to run the race in front of us, to stay on the course God has marked out for us. The race is about being faithful and finishing well.

Unfortunately, we live in an increasingly competitive culture, so comparisons come easily. Sin tempts us to take our eyes off our own children, our own lives, and our own families to compare them to someone else's child, life, or family. Comparing and competing robs our hearts of joyfully trusting God and sacrificially serving our families.

We peek into the lives of others to see how we are measuring up. We look at another mom's home, schedule, clothing, gifts, or children. We compare test scores, athletic accomplishments, or even the spiritual lives of our children. All to see if we (or our children) are "enough." Afraid we might not measure up, we overbook our schedules, become controlling, feel discouraged, or are unnecessarily demanding of our children.

Whether we are driven by hearts of fear or hearts of pride, we must stop comparing and competing if we want to experience the lives God has for us. We need to keep our eyes fixed on Jesus, the author and perfecter of our faith. We need to be in the game and eagerly pursuing faithfulness to God and to our children.

SMALL MOMENTS OF GREATNESS

Our races are often marked by small, rather ordinary moments that actually are big in God's eyes. Moments when we are eye-to-eye and heart-to-heart with our children. When we're not preoccupied with comparing or competing. When we're not thinking about being perfect. When we're not obsessing over how our kids measure up. The greatest moments are when we are present, giving our hearts to God as we give our hearts to this life-changing, gut-wrenching, world-changing work of momming.

In a culture that is dizzy with motion, ambition, information, opportunities, and entertainment, one of the greatest gifts a mom can give her child is her faithful presence. Our homes need a parent's presence more than anything. Presence isn't just about proximity; presence is about purpose. Jesus gives us a beautiful example of this. Notice how he desired to be present with his disciples for the purpose of preparing them: "Jesus went up on a mountainside and called to him those he wanted, and they came to him. He appointed twelve that they might be with him and that he might send them out to preach" (Mark 3:13–14).

Jesus used his presence for the purpose of teaching, loving, preparing, nurturing, modeling, and then, sending. This is so much like the work of being a mom! But let's be honest, sometimes one of the toughest places to be faithfully and fully alive is at home. It's easy to be in close proximity to family, but not be fully present or purposeful. I've been guilty of doing dishes or responding to emails while also half-heartedly trying to answer questions from a curious son or daughter. I've had days where the phone or incoming text messages have stolen more of my attention than necessary. I was home, but not really fully home.

Presence isn't just about proximity; presence is about purpose.

Our children don't need a designer home or even a perfect mom. One of the greatest gifts we can give our children is the gift of ourselves. Present with our time. Present with our attention. What I remember most about my own parents is not whether our car was brand new, whether our food was organic, or if our house was decorated well. I remember being with them.

I remember staying up late talking. Sitting around the table with family. Car rides to a friend's house. Running errands. Working tirelessly side by side on our horse farm. My parents didn't give me perfection. They gave me their time, attention, wisdom, and love. They gave me the gift of themselves. Those snippets of life shared together, small and mundane as they were, were what mattered the most.

So take the pressure off. You aren't always going to be on top of your game. But you can be in it and running your race. Jesus has already met the standard of perfection for you. You can rest in knowing that he alone is perfect. Far more important than always being on your game with gourmet meals, trendy décor, a flawless yard, or creative crafts, is the gift of yourself. Run the race marked out for *you*—and watch what God will do!

CHAPTER 8

No One Appreciates All That I Do!

ow am I going to survive? I thought to myself. It was going to be four-on-one for fourteen days. My husband had just hopped on a plane to California for two weeks of doctoral studies at Biola University. Meanwhile, back in Michigan, I would be flying solo. Four children and an energetic Lab were counting on me.

Choosing to have a positive attitude about the whole situation, I tried to convince myself that maybe this would be a good time to get a lot done. After all, it was summer. Maybe we'd eat out a bit more, head to the pool more often, and keep it simple. And by simple, I was hoping, less busy. In my mind, this would be the perfect opportunity to have fun with the kids, but also work on some writing and catch up on email.

Unfortunately, I had grossly underestimated the impact of going from two parents to one! It wasn't long before I had a whole new level of appreciation for single parents. Our oldest son, Tyler, had recently started working full time at a golf course about twenty minutes from our house. I was getting up at 4:30 a.m. to drop him off, then picking him up in the early afternoon. In between, I was running our kids to dentist appointments, the pool, and friends' houses. Of course by the time everyone was in bed at night I had to go right to bed too to prepare for my early wake-up time of 4:30 a.m. All of the "me" time was getting squeezed out of the schedule.

By day five all I wanted to do was take a nap—all day. We had just gotten back from the pool when Bella said, "Mom, can you take us to Target?" Like her momma, she loves to shop. And she's not an in-and-out kind of girl. Any trip to Target is more like an extended stay. "Not right now," I said to her. "I have been up since 4:30 a.m., we've been at the pool for two hours in ninety-degree heat, and we just went to Target a few days ago," I added.

It all made sense to me. I had given plenty of rationale for why no was a great response. But instead of agreement, my no was met with a silent withdrawal. This is a teen's favorite form of punishment! It was obvious she didn't understand or appreciate all I had been doing. So I went there. Not to Target, but to that place in my heart and mind where I began to feel bad for myself. I threw a private pity party. I quietly wondered, *Why can't they see I am doing this all alone? I wish they would appreciate everything I have done.* And on and on my mind turned. They were honest thoughts, but not overly healthy. Especially for a mom who desires to become better.

This may be one of the most challenging hurdles in momming: the feeling that our children don't appreciate all that we are doing for them. These feelings, as honest as they may be, can wage war against a mom's heart. We spend countless hours of our time and energy that nobody sees. We help with homework. We taxi teens to work, practices, and youth group events. We give gifts, pour out wisdom, listen attentively, play games, and yet somehow, we can feel like everything we do gets sucked into a giant vacuum.

If your feelings have ever invited you to that kind of pity party, the good news is that we don't have to go there. God wants to take those real, raw emotions and use them to turn us toward a deeper kind of love.

THE GREAT IMBALANCE

Like many people, I use the word *love* a lot. Ask any of my friends and they will tell you I am always trying to sell them on something I "love." Not on purpose. It is just a part of who I am. When I love something I have to tell someone else about it! A favorite restaurant. A new clothing store. The best concealer. And so on. But as much as we all use the word *love*, the truth is that we don't always fully understand what real, Christ-like love is. Which is what makes it especially difficult to love our children when they don't appreciate us. So what is love? What is the kind of love that will help us keep giving and serving, even when our hearts are crying, "Doesn't anyone appreciate all that I do?"

One way of thinking about love is to think of it in terms of the object that we are loving. For example, I love Michigan football! As much as my husband and I hate to say goodbye to summer in Michigan, we know that fall and football are on the way. The changing color of the trees, crisp air after muggy summer days, and of course, the town swelling each Saturday for home football games are things we love about fall and football. There are certain qualities of football and fall that are beautiful, good, or pleasing to me, so I say, "I love football."

There is another kind of love though. This kind of love loves not because an object is pleasing or always desirable. It loves out of good will for the benefit of someone else. In momming, we are called to love not for our sakes, but for the benefit of our children. We are to selflessly and sacrificially love them for what God is doing and can do in them. This kind of love seeks the betterment of someone else. This is the kind of love Jesus has toward us.

We love not for our own sakes but for the benefit of our children.

The Bible says that God loved us first (1 John 4:19). In fact, not only did God love us first, but he loved us while we were still a mess. We were still sinners. We were living for ourselves, doing life on our own terms. No thank-you. No appreciation. Yet right in the middle of our sinfulness and selfishness, God loved us anyway.

What makes God's love so different than mine on most days is that he doesn't love me to get anything in return. His love is costly. It is sacrificial. He keeps loving me, knowing full well that I am a work in progress. There is a great imbalance in this love—God loves us far more than we love him. Which is a good reminder as we think about how to love our kids well, even when they don't fully understand or appreciate it.

The truth is, our children will almost always mean more to

us than we will mean to them. I hope that doesn't sound harsh. Think about it this way: God's love for us will always be far greater than our love for him, but it doesn't mean we don't love him, care about him, and do our best to show gratitude toward him. Yet there will always be an imbalance of love because his love for us will always be greater.

How many times do we fail to show thankfulness to God? How often does God have to correct my heart when I fail to be grateful? The answer is, pretty often! But the good news is: God keeps loving me. He doesn't withhold his love from me even when I fail to show how much I appreciate it.

I am learning more and more that the same is true in momming. As parents, we will probably spend far more time loving, serving, and giving to our children than they will ever give back to us. As moms, we will invest far more time in our children than they will likely ever invest in us. It doesn't mean we never tell them no. It doesn't mean we will do whatever they want us to do. But loving in this great imbalance means loving our children for their sakes and not for our own.

When we are tired and worn out after a long day of caring for our children, we can rest our heads easy at night without resentment. When we pour our time and energy into helping a teenage son or daughter work through a difficult friendship, we can have peace knowing we are loving them for their betterment and not our own. When we've stayed up late, helping them figure out difficult homework, it's our awareness of real love that enables us to do it without complaining.

The challenge for any mom in these circumstances is to love anyway. If we are going to become better, more like Christ, then we have to do good even when we feel bad. We have to love even when we feel unloved and underappreciated. When we do, we are moving closer to what it truly means to love and parent like God parents us.

LEARNING TO LOVE THE RIGHT WAY

I have always loved my children. And I am sure you would say the same about yours. Even on our worst days, when we struggle to feel appreciated, we'd all admit we still love our children. But I am learning to love them in the right way. A deeper way. As God is shaping us through this messy mission of momming, let me offer a couple practical ways that move us in the direction of loving our children as God loves us.

Remember that you are shaping them today for what they will be tomorrow (or some day).

For four years our family lived in a small town on the border of Ohio and Indiana. Having spent much of my early childhood in the city and then my college years in Chicago, a rural setting was very different for me. Instead of tall buildings, there were barns. Instead of lots of people, there were lots of cattle. And instead of busy streets, there were fields of corn and soybeans.

It was the first time I truly appreciated the agricultural themes in the Bible. In Mark 4, Jesus talks about a farmer who throws seed (God's Word) on different types of soil (hearts). A farmer works the soil. He tills it, making it suitable for seed to grow. A farmer, at the right time and in the right way, plants seed. He faithfully waters it. And then the farmer watches. And he waits. And waits. There is a lot of work in farming, but there is also a lot of waiting—waiting for the crop to bust its way up through the soil, piercing the surface.

This is what we are doing as moms! Like farmers, we recognize there are different seasons. We are cultivating and preparing our children's hearts. With our life, love, discipline, and the truth of God's Word, we plant. We water. We watch. And we, too, wait.

One of the ways God changes us from the inside out is by reminding us that we are farmers who shouldn't expect too much too soon. I don't mean we lower the bar and throw standards and expectations out the door. What I mean is that we need to remember our children are growing up too. There might be spotty signs of gratitude now, but we must remember to be patient. Growth is a long, slow process. Like a good farmer, we need to abandon our need for immediate results.

Our primary role as moms is preparing, plowing, and planting. This is the work of shaping our children. Or as Proverbs says, "Start children off on the way they should go, and even when they are old they will not turn from it" (22:6). This isn't a guarantee, of course. It's not a promise. But this biblical principle is a reminder that we are to shape and train our children today, because the crop will come "tomorrow." Our goal is to be faithful today while trusting God for the harvest in the hearts of our children.

Don't expect your children to give you what only God can.

In our early years of marriage, I wasn't much of a cook. But over the years I have loved learning and trying new recipes. Recently, I bought a new cookbook with meals that are very different from what our kids are used to. A few weeks ago we were all sitting around the dinner table eating when our younger son, Noah, suddenly blurted out, "Mom, this is so good! Thank you!" Like a row of dominos, the others followed. "Yeah, Mom, this is good. What is it?" One by one, they expressed their delight in my new dish. There is a real sense of satisfaction that comes when the meal I have spent a few hours preparing is appreciated and even better, delighted in! As a mom, I am so grateful for those moments when my children "get it." When they understand why I do what I do for them.

As moms, we should always keep sowing those seeds of thankfulness in our children's hearts, helping them to develop that fruit in their own lives. But as moms, we should never anchor our sense of joy in their love and appreciation. Ultimately, we need to look to God and not our children to fulfill our deepest need for love. It would be great if every time I did something selfless and meaningful for my children, they told me thank you. I wish that every unnoticed act for their sake was met with praise and appreciation. But that's not reality. Not even close! We need to be careful not to expect our children to give us what only God can.

If we look only to our children for a sense of appreciation and approval, we will be met with disappointment. This is why in momming, we must be good receivers before we are good givers. We need to learn to rest in and receive the love God has for us in Christ. We must cling to what God's Word says about us rather than how we feel.

PERFECT LOVE

If we want God's truth to come out of us, we have to put God's truth in us. As the psalmist said, we have to hide God's word in our hearts (Psalm 119:11) so we don't sin against God or those around us. And so recently I memorized 1 John 4:18, "Perfect love drives out fear, because fear has to do with punishment. The one who fears is not made perfect in love." John says the love of Christ is not only good and pleasing, but it is perfect. It is without defect.

It is not hit-or-miss. No matter how I feel, this is what God says about me: I am loved by him.

Looking to someone else, including our children, for love, approval, or appreciation, is a sure sign that we have not yet been "made perfect" in God's love. I'll admit that it is a lifelong struggle to rest securely in the love of our Father, who sent his Son to die for us. God's desire is that we would increasingly experience through the power of the Holy Spirit, "how wide and long and high and deep is the love of Christ" (Ephesians 3:18).

Our children's love for us will always be imperfect. As much as they may express thankfulness and appreciation at times, it will always be lacking in comparison to God's perfect love. What gives us fuel and faith and joy is not *their* love but *God's* love.

One of the ways God changes us and grows us in this season of momming is by increasingly turning us outward as we understand the love of Christ for us and in turn experience his love through us. So the next time you find yourself wondering if anyone appreciates all that you do, the next time you wrestle with feelings of resentment, remember how Jesus loves you. Resist turning inward. With God's help, choose to turn outward. Choose to love anyway, just as God does for you.

CHAPTER 9

I Hate This Stage of Life

A couple years ago our family took a giant leap of faith. In order to start a new church, my husband resigned from his role as the senior pastor of the church where we had been serving. Leaving behind our home, a stable church, and a steady paycheck, we moved to Ann Arbor, Michigan. With four kids, two dogs, and (at the time) a hamster, this was not an easy task.

One of the sacrifices we made was selling our house and moving into a three-bedroom apartment. I kept using the word *cozy* to describe our living conditions. By *cozy* I actually meant small, if not a bit cramped. Who was I kidding?!

Our "cozy" apartment didn't have a basement or attic like our house did. The kids' gathering space was our gathering space. Six of us, plus the dogs, sharing a family room to "hang out" was not always relaxing. Apartment life proved to be a great way to meet new friends for our children, but that also meant our limited space became even more crowded when they invited their new friends over. We had no yard. The kitchen was tight. Everything was smaller, louder, and hotter. Sometimes in the summer, we weren't sure if the air conditioning needed repair or needed a demon exorcised!

What was my solution? I have to confess I hated that stage of life, so I spent a lot of time mentally living somewhere else. The "somewhere else" was a home with our own backyard, room for the kids to run around, a garden, and a kitchen with cabinet space so we didn't have to store some of our pots and pans in our closet. Daydreaming about what I believed was ahead of me seemed like a good idea, but I was missing out on the time right in front of me.

I was missing out on the closeness we enjoyed in that apartment. With limited space, we were together more. I was missing out on the opportunities to get out of the apartment, go for walks, and spend time at the park. There was no need to paint the walls or decorate. This was temporary space for us. Which meant more time for us to enjoy being together.

My choice to check out reminds me of what Frederick Buechner once wrote about "people who get into the habit of thinking their time as not so much an end in itself, a time to be lived and loved and filled full for its own sake, but more as just a kind of way-station on the road to somewhere else."[4]

Ouch! That's what I was doing.

Instead of savoring our time in the present, some of us spend our time living for "somewhere else." When momming turns from fun to frustrating, it is easy to rush through the motions of being a mom without really being present. We declare, "I hate this stage of life!" and instead of making the most of the opportunities in front of us, we look forward to another time. A time when we will have more money or more time or better health;

when the kids will be older and more self-sufficient; when we will have a bigger house or a better car. We look forward to the day when our kids will feed themselves, when they will talk, when they will be capable of using the toilet, when they will be able to stay home alone, when they will drive, or even when they will finally leave home.

It's tempting to want to push the fast-forward button on our lives. Instead of experiencing and enjoying and learning from the time and experiences in front of us, it is easy to wish it away for another day—a quieter, less busy, or more convenient "somewhere else." However, trying to fast-forward to somewhere else is one of many ways we try to escape the hard reality of life as moms.

When I say "escape," I'm not talking about packing your bags in the middle of the night and sneaking out while the kids are asleep to enjoy a week-long vacation on the beach! That's obvious. But escaping is choosing to disengage when life gets hard, and we moms can find many subtle ways to escape, from surfing the web, to watching TV, to working more, to checking our phones. Although there are many ways we try to get through a tough stage by avoiding the reality of momming, is that really what we want?

God wants us to pay attention, to take note, to be "all in." There is more going on when we are moms of young children or energetic teens than just getting through the day. God is inviting us into a different kind of life, a better life, that is characterized by who we are becoming in Christ. When we live for somewhere else or choose other ways of escaping, we can miss what God wants to do in us *right now*. God wants to use all the circumstances of momming to make us more like Christ. When we live for opportunities to escape, it robs us of seeing what God wants to do *today*.

TIME FLIES

My eyes scanned all of the class selections—and it wasn't college classes for me; it was for my son who was entering high school. I wondered, *How can this be happening? How did my baby get to be a freshman in high school?*

The realization hit me like a ton of bricks. It seemed like yesterday that I was seeing my baby for the first time, declaring him to be good and perfect in every way. The last fourteen years flashed before my eyes.

It seems like we just celebrated his first birthday—a memory I'll never forget. The entire family was there. Tyler's eyes were wild with excitement. He wasn't entirely old enough to understand, but he was old enough to know he was at the center of whatever was going on. He looked like a little Smurf, thanks to the blue icing covering his face from his Blue's Clues birthday cake. He was all grins and giggles. I didn't want that day to end any more than he did.

Then, somehow, he was in third grade, no longer batting Wiffle balls around the backyard with my husband. Instead, he was suited up for his first season of baseball. He seemed barely big enough, or strong enough, to swing the bat. Having fun at every turn, he was taking new steps into the world. Steps I knew all too well would eventually take him further from his need for me.

Suddenly, his voice is nearly as deep as my husband's. He shaves. Somehow, he is almost old enough to get his driver's license! He is only a few months away from getting his first real job outside the home. More steps. I wasn't prepared to hold my baby one day and then wake up to register him for high school the next. I wasn't prepared for this. Not one bit.

As I clicked through the schedule choices and all the different tracks he could take based on what he wanted to study in college, an even more sobering thought came to mind. *In just four years he will be on his own. It doesn't even seem possible.* And at this point, I can't even handle the thought.

I know. Everyone warns us that, when it comes to mothering, "The days are long, but the years are short." When we hear it, we politely nod at the well-meaning individuals who feel it is their duty to inform us of the obvious. But I get it now in a way I never did before. I get why I heard so many times and in so many ways, "Just wait, time will fly by."

In this good but strenuous season of being moms, it is easy to lose sight of the time right in front of us. It is going by fast. Our kids are changing. They are growing up. It won't be long before this time will be over, or at least, drastically different. Today is a gift. *Right now* matters.

So we need to be careful of how we live through the challenges of this sometimes boring, often frustrating, and messy time of life. We need to be cautious of wanting to hit the fast-forward button to get past this crazy stage. We need to learn to slow down. Relax. Not worry so much about being—or doing it—perfectly. We live right here. Right now. Not somewhere else.

God is using the changing of diapers, dinnertime, bedtime stories, schooling, and countless other seemingly mundane events of our days to shape our children. But even more than what he has called us to *do* during this season of life, God is graciously using the circumstances and challenges we face to shape who we are *becoming*: better moms.

EMBRACING THE PURPOSE OF MOMMING

A few years ago "The World's Greatest Greeter" began attending our church. He was a hugger. It didn't matter whether he had seen you a hundred times or was meeting you for the first time—he would bellow your name joyfully and then before long you were getting a hug. He embodied the word *embrace*.

To embrace something is to take it in. It is to fully receive or accept. When we embrace something, we open our hearts and lives to receive it. Embracing means we gladly welcome someone or something into our lives. We don't reject or resist it. There is no resisting. There is surrender.

The best thing we can do as moms is to choose to embrace momming—all of it—what we love, what drives us nuts, and what wears us out. And as we embrace momming, we can openly accept that momming has just as much to do with us as it does with raising our kids; God, as a good Father, is also raising us. I'm not just shaping another human being; in Christ and through the power of his Spirit, God is shaping me. The greater purpose is not just about my parenting; the greater purpose is who I am becoming in the process. Seeing God's greater purpose helps us to stay engaged, embracing who God is transforming us into.

Embracing the purpose of momming also opens our eyes and hearts to see the countless learning opportunities right in front of our eyes. Lessons of humility, sacrificial love, and joy. When I think of my own kids, I can't help but see how God has

> *The best thing we can do as moms is to embrace momming—all of it—what we love, what drives us nuts, and what wears us out.*

used each of them to teach me to be brave, patient, kind, fun, more laid back, spontaneous, and willing to dream.

I hope you begin to see why this time of momming is not just to be endured or rushed through, but is to be embraced for God's purpose of making us more like Jesus. We can embrace the truth that just as God is using us to shape our children, God is using the challenges of being a mom to shape us. He is using the small victories, failures, joys, and daunting challenges to make us better.

It's not always easy to embrace momming. In those moments or seasons when it is difficult to welcome with open arms all that God is doing, don't forget that God embraces us. In the mess, he holds us, loves us, cares for us, and sustains us. What he has started in us, he is faithful to finish in us. Even when we can't see the fruit of our labor, he sees clearly who we are becoming. This time is a gift, full of joy and full of trials. But it also has the power to transform.

TRIALS THAT TRANSFORM

I never thought discipline would be harder on me than it is on my children. Learning to teach and train our kids, who are all so different from each other and from me, was and still can be tough. For years, I struggled to understand each child's unique personality and how to discipline in light of it. I was frustrated, and my emotions would spill out. I could see why it would be easier to check out and give in. But slowly and surely, God has used disciplining my children to discipline me. He has humbled me, squeezing the hurry out of this long road of teaching and training our kids. He has helped me to slow down and embrace the journey of motherhood. He's using the hard stuff to grow me. I'm learning to be "compassionate and gracious, slow to anger, abounding in love" (Psalm 103:8). I'm becoming the kind of parent God is to me.

On many occasions, I have had to convince myself of the truth of God's Word when James writes, "Consider it pure joy, my brothers and sisters, whenever you face trials of many kinds, because you know that the testing of your faith produces perseverance. Let perseverance finish its work so that you may be mature and complete, not lacking anything" (James 1:2–4).

God's vision for our lives is maturity. Or as James puts it, God wants us to be complete. The hard stuff has a way of exposing how we are not put together quite yet. We are not whole. This is why our momming often says more about who we are than it does about who our kids are. The pressures, expectations, stress, and loss of control that come along with being a mom can expose our hearts. More importantly, it exposes our need to run to God, the source of lasting change.

How we "consider" or look at the hard stuff determines how we live in it. Here's where our choices begin. What will we do with this good but demanding journey of momming? We can choose to regard this season as a gracious invitation from God to grow. Our kids are not the only ones who are growing up; as moms, we are too.

We must resist the temptation to escape, running from the race God has marked out before us. We must be careful of wanting the easy road. We must value this season for what it really is—good and sacred. It's a chance to increasingly experience the abundant life Jesus talked about. There is a better way—and it starts with a choice. It starts with embracing the work God wants to do in each of us.

As the apostle Paul says, "It is God who works in you to will and to act in order to fulfill his good purpose" (Philippians 2:13). Becoming a better mom starts with becoming a better person. This is the work God is up to. Right now. In this time. At this stage of life. Motherhood is a gift because God is at work in you—even using the challenges of being a mom to shape you into who he wants you to become.

CHAPTER 10

It's Time for Me!

t's not every day that a mom calls it quits and abandons her husband and daughter. When I learned it had happened, I was as shocked as anyone else who knew her. From the outside, she was a pretty normal mom. She went to church. She served in the community. She worked hard at her job. Married for several years, she had one child and one on the way. Everything seemed good. She even seemed happy.

Then, suddenly, she was done. Everything unraveled. The way she described it, she simply had had enough. Enough of marriage. Enough of parenting. Enough of doing what everyone else wanted her to do. It was time to take care of herself. Her past had been about others—their needs, expectations, desires, and dreams. Her future was going to be different.

With the goal of seeking the "good life," she stepped out of the life she had been building to start a life that revolved around her and what she wanted. Fortunately, her extreme choice—the epitome of a self-centered life—is not the norm. But while her actions aren't too common, her attitude is far more prevalent than you might think. In lesser ways, many moms live a life that says, "It's time for *me*!" And popular cultural messages often encourage us to indulge ourselves.

For example, a frequent response to the challenges and responsibilities of momming is to check out. After all, everyone has a breaking point, so do what you want to do! Indulge yourself. Forget about trying to be a better mom; just put on a movie for the kids, lock yourself in the bathroom, and gorge yourself with all the dark chocolate you can find! Some books, blogs, and movies even glorify the messiness of momming and encourage moms to do whatever feels good, even to the extreme of justifying or glamorizing "bad" moms.

And let's face it. If we're honest, most of us struggle with some of these emotions and attitudes to a certain degree. I mean, who doesn't like the idea of doing what we want to do? I wouldn't trade my kids for anything. I love being a wife and mom. But there are moments when it would be nice to have a day—okay, a week—when I could sit and enjoy a cup of coffee without having to grab breakfast for the kiddos, take the dog outside, and clean up the glass of milk that spilled onto the floor. Or wouldn't it be nice not to have to think about homework, soccer schedules, or recitals, let alone the kids' manners, character, and attitudes?

In many seemingly harmless ways, we envision the "good life" as a life that revolves around getting what we want, when we want it, and how we want it. The problem is, our vision of the good life—a life that is all about us—is not the life God invites us into.

Jesus came to give us life, and life to the full (John 10:10). The good life Jesus offers isn't a life we naturally choose or can obtain on our own. Jesus transforms us to live for God and others rather than for ourselves. It's a life in which we become better as we learn to see true greatness and fulfillment in focusing less on ourselves. The paradox of the good life is that when we lose the life we think we want, we actually find it (Matthew 10:38–39).

Although taking care of ourselves may seem fulfilling, the sin of selfishness is deceiving. The truth is, we weren't made to live a self-serving life that pushes God and others aside. We were created to live life with and for God. We were created to find true fulfillment in living for the benefit of others.

REDEFINING THE "GOOD LIFE"

Even Jesus's earliest followers, his disciples, got this mixed up. They too had a vision for the good life—a life that had them at the center instead of others. But Jesus had a different idea. Jesus makes it clear to his disciples that true fulfillment does not come from where they thought it would.

The passage in John 10 begins with Jesus and his disciples heading to Jerusalem. "They were on their way up to Jerusalem, with Jesus *leading the way* . . ." (Mark 10:32, emphasis mine). Remember that phrase, "leading the way." Underline it. Highlight it. Circle it. Do whatever you need to do to remember it. It is important: Jesus leads, we follow.

As they walked, the brothers James and John came to Jesus with a ridiculous request: "Teacher ... we want you to do for us whatever we ask" (Mark 10:35).

Say what?! Can you imagine telling God, "We want you to serve us"? They are in effect saying, "It's all about me! Give us what we want!"

In grace, Jesus asks the two brothers what they want. What

they want is to be front and center—with Jesus, of course. They want to sit one on the right and one on the left of Jesus. They are asking for places of honor, recognition, worship, and glory. Jesus reminds them that this is not why he has come and that it's not the abundant life he brings. The good life Jesus offers is very different from what the disciples imagined. It is not about living for ourselves; it is found in dying to ourselves. So Jesus says, "For even the Son of Man did not come to be served, but to serve, and to give his life as a ransom for many" (Mark 10:45).

In the disciples' minds, they were on their way to Jerusalem because they thought Jesus was about to make a grand entrance. They thought Jesus would finally defeat their enemies and establish his kingdom on earth. Victory would be theirs! But Jesus wasn't going to Jerusalem to be celebrated; he was going to be crucified. He wasn't establishing a political kingdom on earth; he was establishing a spiritual kingdom in our hearts.

Please don't overlook the weight of this interaction. Jesus is not just contrasting two different ways of life; he is *inviting* them to a different way of life—to follow the way he lived, to follow his words and actions. The only way we get to experience the good life Jesus offers is by letting him lead the way and trusting that he is worth following. The world values a life of greatness and fulfillment in the form of power, fame, wealth, taking care of yourself, indulging, and doing whatever you want. But in God's kingdom a valuable life is found in becoming a Christ-like servant—one who lives and gives for the benefit of others.

There are, of course, things we need to do to nourish our souls. But despite what we may be led to believe, happiness and fulfillment are not found in living for ourselves. Jesus invites us to experience something better. Real life, lasting impact, and true greatness are found in forgiving, loving the unlovable, walking in humility, doing small things nobody sees, having a willingness to sacrifice, and giving instead of always looking to receive.

I CAN'T DO IT!

Recently, Patrick called our family together and announced, "Kids, we're going to memorize Matthew 22:37–39." And he began to read Matthew's words: "Jesus replied: 'Love the Lord your God with all your heart and with all your soul and with all your mind.' This is the first and greatest commandment. And the second is like it: 'Love your neighbor as yourself.'"

Getting a little excited, Patrick began to preach—I mean explain—how the two greatest commandments were to love God and love one another. He told us, "Every day we have many choices of who and what we are going to love. We will either love God and others or we will love ourselves. If our hearts are ruled by our own comfort or pleasure or by wanting to be in charge or to be right, then those desires will rule our lives."

Finally, our oldest daughter, Bella, looking a little defeated, couldn't take any more. She chimed in, "Nobody is perfect, Dad! I can't do it."

Silence. Then Patrick said, "That's exactly the point. You can't. You won't. None of us are perfect. Which is why we need Jesus to help us love God and love others."

Our daughter is right. And so is Patrick. We can't love and follow Jesus on our own. The good life Jesus offers us is never one we can live in our own strength. We need his help.

When we are struggling—when the burden of giving, the burden of living for others gets heavy—the temptation is to try harder. But that would be starting in the wrong place. Our hearts are not changed by trying harder or by doing better. We'll never be able to live for others in our own strength. The strength to follow Jesus is not from us; the source is Jesus's life in us through the power of his Spirit. This is why we are to "walk by the Spirit" so that that we won't "gratify the desires of the flesh" (Galatians 5:16). What makes loving God and loving one another possible is the power God gives us as we rely on him.

The good life is not about seeking our own way; it is about Jesus leading the way. God's grace, the truth of his Word, and the power of his Spirit enable us to know and see what Jesus has done for us. The power to be a servant is not found in us; the power to be a servant is found in Christ, the greatest servant, who by faith lives in us and empowers us to follow his example.

> *The good life is not about seeking our own way; it is about Jesus leading the way.*

When we come to him in faith and receive his love and forgiveness as unworthy recipients, it changes us. As we keep coming to his Word and opening our hearts to him, he continually changes us. The good life, lived perfectly only by Jesus, changes us from being self-centered to being selfless.

Growing in Jesus isn't just a lifelong process; it's a lifelong relationship that is changing us for the better. Growing in Jesus enables us to do what the apostle Paul says in 2 Corinthians

5:15: "He died for all, that those who live should no longer live for themselves but for him who died for them and was raised again." This life, marked by living for others, is not just a *good* life. It's a *better* life.

THIS IS SO MUCH BETTER . . .

As I tucked one of my kids in late one evening, I quietly thought to myself, *This is better.* The quiet moments of snuggling, reading, and talking about God with my children are so much better than anything else I could have imagined for myself.

Just a few nights later, my husband and I sat on the bed next to our son. We talked about college, which is only a few years away. We talked about how choices build character and character is like strong walls that protect a city. We talked about wisdom, purity, and how to live for more than yourself.

Were we tired? Yes! Were we ready to relax on the couch for some time for just the two of us? Absolutely. But once again I thought, *This is so much better.*

The life I have found in Jesus, the life he is giving me and I am giving to others, is so much better than self-indulgence. It's better than accolades at work. It's better than thousands of shares on a blog, article, status, or video. A life lived for others is better than more money in the bank. It's better than more time to ourselves. It's better than the easy road.

In the end, this giving of ourselves is the stuff that lasts. This life of giving, loving, serving, and dying to ourselves as we follow the example of Jesus our Savior really is the good life.

CHAPTER 11

I Hate to Fail

I stood in the kitchen counting: one, two, three, four, and on until I reached twenty. "Ready or not, here I come!" I yelled.

The kids and I were in our second, or maybe third, round of an intense game of hide-and-seek. At the time, they were pretty young, and experience was on my side. Our creaky wooden floors worked to my advantage, providing helpful clues for identifying where each child was attempting to hide.

I could hear one of them in the downstairs family room, not so quietly trying to hide behind our TV. The other three? I could hear them scrambling for secret places and dark spaces upstairs. I heard one in our bathroom. Another one in the hallway closet. And another child was no doubt in the girls' bedroom.

One by one, I found them. Tyler was in the family room. Bella, the bathroom. Noah was squeezed behind a floor mop and a bucket in the hallway closet. And Sophia, our youngest? If she hadn't moved, I would likely find her in the girls' bedroom.

As I entered their bedroom, I could see a rather noticeable "blob" in the middle of the room. The girls' bunkbeds flanked one wall and several dressers lined another. And right out in the open, huddled under a blanket, was Sophia—hiding—in full view! You should have seen the look of surprise on her face when I gently pulled the blanket off, exposing her secret hiding place. Apparently, she thought if she couldn't see me, then I couldn't see her.

The truth is, most of us are pretty good at trying to hide what is really happening in our hearts. The bad news is, our attempts to do so are about as effective as Sophia's—obvious to everyone but us! As painful as it may be, we all need to experience the confusion and shock of having the blanket pulled off our hiding places.

That is exactly what momming does. God graciously uses momming to uncover what is going on inside our hearts to help us become better by becoming more like Christ. But first we have to come out of hiding.

OUR KIDS TELL US THE TRUTH ABOUT OURSELVES

One morning my nerves were wearing thin. It was one of those days when I had awakened on the wrong side of the bed. As the morning wore on and the overall volume of my house increased, I became more and more impatient and irritable, and less and less like Jesus. I was responding to my kids' requests with short, terse answers. I was nagging them about every little thing that was wrong or out of place. After becoming increasingly upset by all the messes and really frustrated by the overwhelming tasks of the day, I noticed that Bella hadn't cleaned the bathroom as I had asked.

That was it! My voice rose as I tried to hold back my irritation. I listed off to her all the tasks she still needed to do and how she had better "get going." I let her know there was too much to do to just mosey around and take her sweet old time.

When I saw the hurt look on her face, I knew I had crossed the line. My behavior had been a bit overboard, and I immediately felt the sting of conviction. Realizing my own sin, I backed off and sheepishly apologized. As a mom I had blown it, even if it was just for a moment.

I had crossed the line. It was clear to me that I did not measure up. And I hated the fact that I had failed.

I wanted to go back into hiding. But exposing our flaws is one of the ways God can make us better. It's how he works. So if this feels all too familiar to you, don't despair. God uses momming to uncover the places in our hearts that need his grace and truth the most.

The Bible says, "Nothing in all creation is hidden from God's sight. Everything is uncovered and laid bare before the eyes of him to whom we must give account" (Hebrews 4:13). God sees it all. The good, the bad, and the ugly. We may try with all our might, but there is nothing we can hide from God!

God shows us who we are so we can learn to depend on who he is.

Consider, for example, how Adam and Eve first responded to their sin in the Garden of Eden. They didn't listen to their wise and loving Father. God had told them they were free to eat from any of the trees in the Garden except for one—the tree of the knowledge of good and evil (Genesis 2:16–17). And just like little kids, they decided that was exactly the one tree they wanted to eat from.

Instead of trusting God, they wanted to *be* God. So they did what they wanted and the consequences were deadly. Sin left its mark. And all of creation still feels the effects of that first act of disobedience.

Adam and Eve responded to their first awareness of falling short by trying to hide (Genesis 3:8). Instead of running *to* God, they ran *from* God. How much easier, and better, if they had come out of hiding to find God's grace in their time of need. Instead, they ran from the very One who is the source of truth, love, and healing.

So hiding is as old as the Garden of Eden. And just like our ancestral parents, we too become experts in hiding. We minimize our sin, defend it, pretend it's not there, excuse it, or just plain deny it. But God is not fooled. Nothing is hidden from his sight.

MESSED UP

God is not the only one who sees our sin. Our kids see it too. That's the way momming works. Our kids have a unique way of pointing out our weak spots. All the grand ideas we had about ourselves get kicked down and uncovered. The pleasant visions we had of being a patient, sacrificial, always caring, and untiring mom get wrecked not by our kids, but by our own sin.

It's not that we are never patient or kind; it's that in the middle of momming we discover we are in worse condition than we ever imagined. Our hearts are not pure. Our motives are not always good. Our identities are not always anchored in God's love for us. Our kids help break down the false ideas of how close to perfect we think we are and reveal that there is a lot of work yet to be done—from the inside out!

But please don't be discouraged by the process. God isn't just using us to shape our kids; he uses our kids to help tell us the truth about who we are and how far we have to go. And remember, even when the process feels awful, God is not doing it to defeat us but to provide us real and lasting transformation. What needs changing first is not our husbands, our kids, or our homes, but our own hearts.

Being made aware of our own brokenness is painful. The pain a mom feels when she fails is not only for herself but for her child as well. I am reminded of my friend who called one day to ask what we did when our kids didn't respond to no at an early age.

"I just don't want to do the wrong thing and mess up my child," she said. In her mind, messing up as a mom meant messing up her child. Many moms carry that fear. As moms we carry an unnecessarily heavy load when we try to do everything perfectly and try to get everything right. But no one can carry that load for long. Failure is inevitable in momming.

There are countless decisions we make over the course of our children's lives. Some are small and some are big. We make choices about discipline, diet, sports, friends, church, college, dating, and we even influence our kids as they are choosing a future spouse. Yikes! It's no wonder our hearts become heavy or fearful as we seek to wisely navigate these treacherous waters. It's no wonder our hearts feel burdened and sometimes broken when we don't get it right.

Sometimes our feelings of failure are accurate. We do miss the mark. We say things or do things we shouldn't. God humbles us. Our hearts get exposed. Our failures might require us to pause for reflection and confession. Our shortcomings and mistakes can provide great opportunities to move in a new and better direction. Our failures, whether big or small, are opportunities for God to do some much-needed work in our hearts.

THE HEART OF THE PROBLEM IS A PROBLEM WITH THE HEART

Jesus spent so much time talking about the heart because becoming a better mom, a better person, requires digging deep to get beneath all the ways we try to hide. Just as a gardener cultivates the soil to prepare it to properly receive seed, Jesus needs to cultivate our hearts.

A move to a new town and a few hosta plants reminded me just how much our hearts are the real heart of the problem. I have always loved gardening. Pulling weeds, not so much! When my husband and I bought our first house, we made a pact that he would do the heavy lifting of digging new beds and planting. I would do the work of watering.

Let me just say, I ended up on the good side of that agreement. For nearly ten years it worked well. Then, due to a job change, we moved to a new town nearly an hour away. We had a different house and, as we would find out, completely different soil conditions.

Our first house had soft, rich, and sandy soil. It was the kind of "good soil" Jesus talked about. In Mark 4:3–9, he talks about a farmer who goes out and throws seed on four different types of soil. The seed illustrates God's Word and the soils are different types of hearts. Jesus says:

"Listen! A farmer went out to plant some seed. As he scattered it across his field, some of the seed fell on a footpath, and the birds came and ate it. Other seed fell on shallow soil with underlying rock. The seed sprouted quickly because the soil was shallow. But the plant soon wilted under the hot sun, and since it didn't have deep roots, it died. Other seed fell among thorns that grew up and choked out the tender plants so they produced no grain. Still other seeds fell on fertile soil, and they sprouted, grew, and produced a crop that was thirty, sixty, and even a hundred times as much as had been planted!" Then he said, "Anyone with ears to hear should listen and understand." (NLT)

The soil at our old house was the good or "fertile soil." It wasn't hard, shallow, or full of weeds. It was the kind of soil that provided the right environment for growth. But that was not the kind of soil at our new house.

I'll never forget looking out the window the day after Patrick had planted four brand new hostas in the backyard mulch bed. They looked beautiful, full, and strong when we brought them home. The next day they looked like they had just lost their best friend. Wilted. Droopy. Sad. They were well on their way to dying.

We had done exactly what we had done at the old house. Same plants. Same landscaping designs. Same plant food. Same tools. We hadn't changed anything. The only difference was the soil. In our new home the soil was dense, hard clay. By itself, that soil was nothing close to ideal for growing anything. Nothing planted in it stood a chance of living. The soil needed transformation.

When it comes to life and growth, soil matters! This is exactly Jesus's point in the parable. Having the right kind of soil (heart) is important if we are going to produce abundant and fruitful lives. So if we want the kind of hearts that produce a "harvest of thirty, sixty, or even a hundred times as much as had been planted" (Mark 4:20 NLT), our hearts need transformation. Just as our hard, clay soil needed amending with organic matter, we also need to amend our hardened hearts with God's truth and love, so that through the power of God's Spirit, we experience more fruitful lives for God's kingdom.

DYING IN ORDER TO TRULY LIVE

Unfortunately, the path toward life sometimes feels like death. To begin cultivating good hearts, we need to be honest about the emotions that control our hearts. Which of us really wants to feel angry, anxious, irritable, or overwhelmed? These emotions can get the better of us, impacting our homes and families. But if we want to become better moms and experience the abundant lives Jesus promised, we need to put to death our sinful desires, which can lead to these negative emotions. We need to admit that these emotions often expose what is inside our hearts. We need to own, confess, and repent of the wrong desires that can so easily take up residence in our hearts, leaving us to feel the way we often do.

In his booklet *Conflict*, Timothy Lane offers a helpful outline of common desires that can turn into self-centered demands. Do any of these sound familiar?

> Comfort. I want, must have, and deserve some rest and relaxation, and you'd better not hinder my ability to get it!
>
> Approval. I want, must have, and deserve your approval, and you'd better give it to me!

Success. I want, must have, and deserve to be successful, and I'll do anything to achieve it.

Power. I want, must have, and deserve power, and I will do anything to have it.[5]

There have been times where the desire of my heart was for the easy path. I was looking for a more comfortable journey through momming, one we all know doesn't exist. The emotions of anger or irritation were showing me that I was serving myself more than I was serving God and my family. At other times, all the tough work of momming slowly settled into my heart as emotions of self-pity and resentment. Didn't anyone else see all I was doing? Once again, God graciously and gently exposed how my heart desired approval and respect from my spouse or kids instead of from God. Digging into the heart can be messy! But it's where real and lasting change happens.

Sometimes, though, my negative emotions were not so much an expression of my selfish desires as they were a flashing signal that something needed to change in our household, or that an issue needed to be addressed with my children. Was I overwhelmed with housework? Maybe it was time to teach the kids some new chores. Was I irritable at how ungrateful the children seemed? Perhaps I needed to focus on teaching them (yet again!) how to say thank you and how to be thankful for all that we have. Was I angry at my teen for spending too much time on his cell phone? Maybe he needed a reminder of the distraction screen time can be and some pointers on putting boundaries in place. Of course, once I identify the issue, I still need God's help to address it with wisdom and patience.

One of the primary problems of our hearts (and our

parenting!) is that we try to do life apart from God. We resist him. We live out of our own strength and power instead of by the power of his Spirit. We want our way instead of God's will. We allow our feelings and desires to become the most important thing to us—more important than teaching our children or following Christ. We have to die to ourselves in order to come alive to Jesus and all that he wants us to do to shape our kids for the future.

But to become better moms by becoming more like Christ, we need to be honest with where we are. God shows us who we are so we can learn to depend on who he is. You see, we were made to be in relationship with God. We were made to walk with him, trust him, and live lives that glorify him. A relationship with the Father and the Son by the Spirit is life-giving and nourishing.

But to get there, we have to come out of hiding. We have to admit where we are so we can move closer to where God wants us to be. It's interesting that the very first question God asks that is recorded in the Bible is found in the Garden—shortly after Adam and Eve went into hiding. Of course, God knew exactly where they were. But still he kindly asks, "Where are you?" It's a question God is asking each of us. He invites us to consider where we really are.

David modeled this life of soul searching in the presence of God: "Search me, God, and know my heart; test me and know my anxious thoughts. See if there is any offensive way in me, and lead me in the way everlasting" (Psalm 139:23–24). God wants us to work with him; he wants us to *invite* him to lay our lives bare before him, to search out the offensive, hidden parts of our hearts, to deal with those areas, and then to follow him into a life that lasts—eternally.

God gives us an invitation to walk out of hiding and admit our brokenness—not to stay there, but to grow there. Our brokenness is always an invitation into God's grace. He is saying to us, "Come out of hiding. Stop running. Give up. Don't try to do this on your own. Come to me, the source of real life. I have something better for you."

God wants to give us good hearts; hearts that are being renewed by his Spirit. He wants hearts that are soft, humble, teachable, and increasingly fruitful. God longs for not just an external conformity to rules but an inner alignment of our hearts with his will. It's a heart that says, "Lord, here am I. Do what you want in me and through me. These kids are yours. I am yours. Don't just change my kids, change all of me. Make me an instrument that is holy and noble for purposes beyond what I can always see or understand."

As we learn to trust him and surrender our lives to him, we will gradually experience the abundant life of loving God and neighbor—a life of decreasing anxiety, fear, self-centeredness, and discontentment. We will begin to experience lives that naturally bring about love, joy, peace, patience, kindness, goodness, faithfulness, gentleness, and self-control. We will learn that even our failures help us to be *better*—with God's help.

CHAPTER 12

I Worry Constantly

everal years ago our family loaded up the car and headed south to the beautiful mountains of Kentucky. When we arrived, we had some downtime at the lodge where we were staying. With four kids who had managed to survive an eight-hour car ride, some activity was a must!

I wasn't excited about my husband's choice of activity, however. I was hoping for the pool. Shopping. Or at the very least, a movie. *Not* hiking. But once my husband had suggested it, the decision was made.

"Come on, Mooooooom!" one child begged.

"We've been in a car all day," another argued.

"I want to see a bear!" one child pleaded.

"Exactly!" I said. "That is exactly why I do *not* want to go for a hike."

It was late in the day, I was being a "mother bear" myself, and I was keenly aware of it. We would soon be losing daylight, the kids were losing patience, and I was losing the argument. So off we went. My husband, our four kids, and I started off on a wooded trail. In the mountains. Did I mention it was getting dark?

Everything inside me disagreed with Pat's decision. Fear settled on this momma as the deeper into the trail we went, the darker it got. I was used to trails in Michigan. Flat. Safe. There was nothing flat about this trail. For me, the rocky ledges, deep valleys, and hilly terrain were too much—more like a recipe for disaster than an impromptu hiking adventure!

Which is why we all screamed when Bella began to slip. It wasn't a sudden drop. It was more like a slow-motion slide. But if Pat had not grabbed her by the hair, the fall would have ended poorly.

But Pat caught her. Held her. Safely. By his hand. In the middle of unfamiliar terrain. Out in the woods. On the edge of darkness. The safest place my daughter could be in that moment was in her father's hand. It was a lesson I have never forgotten, a lesson that went far beyond the moment.

OUR LIFE IS IN HIS HANDS

I often worry about my children. Will they make the right choices? Will they grow up to love God? How will they handle peer pressure? The list goes on and on. But the good news is, my children are in the hands of God. Whether I can always keep them safe, happy, and successful is beside the point. The God who created my children and entrusted them to me will not let them out of his grasp. The safest place on earth is in God's hands. And that's true for me too.

The psalmist said: "I've put my life in your hands. You won't drop me, you'll never let me down" (Psalm 31:5 MSG). We find similar reminders that we are safe in God's hands in Psalm 139:

"You hem me in behind and before, and you lay your *hand* upon me" (v. 5, emphasis added). And "If I rise on the wings of the dawn, if I settle on the far side of the sea, even there your *hand* will guide me, your right *hand* will hold me fast" (vv. 9–10, emphasis added).

In each of these examples, we see the confidence and peace that comes from knowing that our lives are in God's hands. Like an affectionate parent, God has set his hand upon us. His hand will guide us and hold us fast—strongly and with security.

The truth of God's Word reminds us that even when we are afraid, God is in control. Our lives are in his hands. For moms, learning to release control is hard, but it is good for our hearts. As scary as letting go can be, I am encouraged by the story of one mom in the Bible who had to learn the same lesson—in far scarier circumstances than mine.

A MOM WHO HAD TO LET GO

The story of Moses's mom is found in the book of Exodus. She lived in Egypt, a descendent of the Israelites who had left Canaan because of a great famine. Originally, the Egyptians had looked favorably on the Israelites, but at the beginning of Exodus we learn that a new king of Egypt arose who was no friend of the Israelites. Among other oppressive and harmful decrees, he gave orders to kill all the newborn Hebrew boys.

But Moses's mom was no wimp. Neither were a few brave Hebrew midwives. They feared God more than they feared Pharaoh. Instead of killing Moses at birth, they saved him. Eventually, the day came when Moses's mom could not hide or hold him any longer. She had to let him go—praying, hoping, trusting that the hand of God would save him.

Can you imagine what Moses's mom must have felt? She put her son in a basket, and slowly opened her hands, releasing him to the waters of the mighty Nile—the very place Pharaoh had ordered the midwives to throw all newborn Hebrew boys to die. She had to let go of her child, but God did not.

This story is even more meaningful to me because of its connection to another familiar story from earlier in the Bible about a man named Noah. To bring judgment on the wicked, God was going to send a flood. But out of God's grace and mercy, he chose to save the righteous Noah by instructing him on how to build an ark. As Ravi Zacharias observes, God supplied "every detail of the ark: how high, how wide, what kind of wood—the comprehensive blueprint. Yet two details are conspicuously absent: no sail and no rudder. Imagine preparing to float on water for that many days with nothing to control the direction of the ship!"[6]

Now return to the story about Moses's mother in Exodus 2:3: "But when she could hide him no longer, she got a papyrus basket for him and coated it with tar and pitch. Then she placed the child in it and put it among the reeds along the bank of the Nile."

The Hebrew word *tevah* that was used for *basket* in Exodus 2:3 is the same word used in Genesis 6:14 for *ark*! Just as Noah built a *tevah* with no sail or rudder, Moses's mom placed her son in a miniature *tevah*. Her act of faith was clear. Her God was the creator and covenant-keeping God of Israel. She didn't have to be in control because God was! So she acted not in despair but in defiance because she knew who really controlled all of history, including the future of her children.

Many times life leaves us feeling as if we are in a ship without a rudder. We feel the uncertainty and fear of being caught up in the current or being tossed back and forth amid the wind and waves. That's when it can be helpful to remember Noah and Moses. Even though they were each in a *tevah*, presumably without a sail or rudder, God was firmly in control of the ark and of those inside.

An anxious heart and constant worry might look like good parenting on the outside, but underneath it reveals a heart that doesn't fully trust God. God alone controls the future. From the very beginning of the Bible, God has wanted and tried to get us to trust him.

There comes a point when we have to realize our children are ultimately under the protection and provision of God. Nothing can free our hearts from excessive and unnecessary worry like trust and confidence in him. This does not excuse us from teaching, providing, and protecting, but it does release us from the burden of trying to be God.

ADMITTING OUR LIMITATIONS

Nothing in life takes God by surprise. Nothing has, or will, come into the lives of our families by accident. Although Moses's mom had plenty to be fearful of and a lot she was responsible for, she knew who controlled the future. She knew the safest place to be was in God's hands. As she trusted him, she discovered that God is good, faithful, and in control.

The God who created my children and entrusted them to me will not let them out of his grasp.

When we don't trust God, we will inevitably try to be God. It is a useless endeavor. We can never be all-knowing, all-powerful, or ever-present. We are made in the image of God, but we can never be God. Only he knows and understands all things. His strength is perfect and unending. As much as we try to be everywhere, at the same time, doing everything we can to provide everything everybody needs, it never works!

There is freedom in admitting our limitations. The sooner we not only realize, but rest in that truth, the better. Psalm 103:14 says, "For he knows how we are formed, he remembers that we are dust." We won't always be able to be there for our kids. We can't be omniscient, omnipotent, or omnipresent. Those attributes belong to God alone.

Instead of letting our worries and fears run us into the ground, we should use them to push us into our Father's arms, as we run to him to find our peace and security. Psalm 103:13 says, "As a father has compassion on his children, so the LORD has compassion on those who fear him." When it comes to the fate and future of our children, there is nothing to fear. We can trust in the one who orders each step.

CHAPTER 13

Motherhood Is Robbing Me of _____

I was trying to get my headset on—the one I was using to answer the phone for my dad's business. "Hello, this is Ruth, how can I help you?" I said.

My dad was a home inspector, and to make money from home, I went to work scheduling appointments for his company. The job was pretty simple. Plus, I absolutely loved it because I got to interact with people all the time.

We had converted our kitchen pantry into a home office, what would more appropriately be called a cloffice (closet-office). It was small, but functional. The shelves we used to put canned goods on were now used for storing folders, business cards, and pamphlets to send out to customers and real estate agents. The new setup seemed like it would be perfect for juggling work as a mom. I would soon discover that the task was not as easy as it seemed, especially when trying to take care of a baby and schedule appointments at the same time!

For several months, working at home went well. I was hugely pregnant so I appreciated the short "commute" from upstairs to downstairs. Then I gave birth. *No problem,* I thought. *Newborns sleep a lot, right?*

But there was a problem. Our newborn didn't stay "new" for very long. He began to make noise and make frequent requests. He was always on the move. Keeping him in one place proved to be a full-time job in and of itself—which is why I was wearing a headset to answer phones. But too often I was trying to get my headset on when the phone rang and Tyler would be crying from the other room. I was torn. I was trying to do work I loved and do it well. I was also trying to be a mom and do that well.

It didn't take long to make the decision. The pantry that had become an office became a laundry room. My "work" was changing. No more sales, no more crunching numbers, no more interacting with people. Being a mom to Tyler needed more of my time and attention than I could give while working for my dad. A little reluctantly, I said goodbye to working from home—not only goodbye to working, but goodbye to things that had given me energy, purpose, and a sense of accomplishment. I didn't regret being a mom, but I felt like I was missing out on something.

LOSING "ME" IN MOMMING

During the early years, the "honeymoon phase" of momming fueled me. I attacked motherhood with enthusiasm. I read books, took walks, changed diapers, tucked our kids in each night, and thoroughly cherished those moments. But as time went on, I couldn't shake the sense that I was missing out. It wasn't that I didn't love being a mom or love my kids. It was a quiet but nagging belief that I had in some way given up a lot to be a mom. This new season of life, which I considered beautiful and sacred, was keeping me from other things I once enjoyed.

I struggled with the realization that momming meant more alone time and less adult time. Being a mom was taking away time from some of the friendships I once enjoyed and desperately needed. I felt tired. The schedule was busier. My friends who didn't have kids were gone all day, so I couldn't connect with them. Momming began to create distance and isolation from relationships I valued and needed.

Momming was a sacrifice financially too. We wrestled with how we would live on a pastor's income. I was no longer contributing financially to our family. I felt like I was giving up control of my future, professionally and financially, as I became solely dependent on my husband.

When I was in retail sales, it was crystal clear to me what success and failure looked like. Goals were definable and measurable. The outcomes of my work were easy to see and evaluate. Not so much with momming. My gauge for "success" disappeared about as quickly as a gallon of milk does with four kids in the house. I discovered that measuring success as a mom wasn't easy. I was shaping, nurturing, and teaching a child, hoping what I was doing was actually right. Many days it felt like I was shooting in the dark.

Even in the area of ministry, momming changed what I could give. I had spent countless hours as a co-laborer and partner with my husband in youth ministry. We'd invite kids over, take kids out, stay up late, and do it all again the next week. And we were in it together. All of this became more difficult when I became a mom because I had less time and energy to give to it. I felt guilty.

At times, I felt frustrated. And many times I felt alone. Momming, so I thought, was robbing me of doing "God's work." Little did I realize at the time that my ministry was right in front of me.

I'M *JUST* A MOM?

Somehow, I had bought into the myth that I was "just a mom." It seemed that being a mom was robbing me of money, meaning, and more important work. I felt like I was "less than" who I was. It seemed even the simple interactions of daily life conspired to remind me of what I had lost.

One day I stopped by the bank to make a deposit and update our personal information. Everything was fine until the teller asked me for my place of employment. That's a question I always struggle to answer. Where do I start?

I am the creator of several ministry websites.

I am a blogger.

I am a speaker.

I write books.

But . . . I am also a mom.

Scrambling to find a simple, one-word answer, I finally blurted out, "I am a homemaker." This really threw the young teller for a loop!

"It's *all* you do?" she asked. Not only could I see the confused and even critical look on her face, I could feel it. To clarify, she continued, "Okay, so you are *just* a stay-at-home mom?" I heard all of her words, but it was the word *just* that stuck to me like an unwanted glob of mascara. I didn't know whether to laugh or cry!

"Ummmm, well, I *am* a mom," I stated.

"If you ever start working, we can update your information," the teller stated matter-of-factly.

"'Ever start working?" I muttered to myself. I was fighting back words, still trying to comprehend what I just heard.

To make matters worse, the teller *still* wasn't done! One last time she said, "Okay, so that is all you do?"

In order to avoid a war of words, I left it at that. I don't believe she was trying to be mean or had anything against moms. Her response, though, illustrates a typical attitude in our culture. I had struggled with the same feelings. No matter whether you are a stay-at-home mom, a work-from-home mom, or a work-outside-the home mom, the feeling of *just* being a mom is prevalent. It's easy to fall into thinking that being a mom isn't "real" work. That it is somehow less valuable, significant, or worthwhile in comparison to other pursuits.

No wonder one of the most common feelings a woman faces when she has children is the feeling of "missing out" or feeling "less than." If we aren't careful, the sense that something valuable has been taken from us can leave us feeling discouraged, frustrated, or even resentful. But like all lies, it must be fought with the truth.

Sometimes the wake-up call to what matters most happens when we hear our kids pray for the first time. Sometimes it happens late at night, talking to our teenage sons or daughters about what they are wrestling with. Sometimes it comes in the minivan on the way to the store. The sacred, life-shaping work of raising another human being *is* real work—and it's right in front of us!

And just because our kids are growing up doesn't mean this battle of the heart goes away. Even now, as my kids are growing up too quickly, I need the reminder, so well stated by Andy Stanley, "Your greatest contribution to the kingdom of God might not be something you do but someone you raise."[7]

At different times and in different ways, God has reminded me of what kind of ambition matters most. Our greatest ambition is not getting the next promotion, the next sale, or another paycheck. Our greatest ambition is raising up another generation of children to live for God's glory and the good of the world. As moms, we are not just getting by. We are fulfilling God's mission and purpose by shaping kids today for the sake of the world tomorrow.

Not only do we need to recapture the vision for what we're doing, we need to remember who God is inviting us to become in the process. *What* we are doing counts both outside the home and inside the home, but *who* we are becoming is just as important.

REFINING, NOT ROBBING

There is no question that momming changes what we can and cannot do. We have to rearrange our priorities and pursuits for sure. We have to work harder at making time for us and not neglecting the important things we love to do. We have to carve out time and be more intentional about friendships, hobbies, and activities that refuel us as moms. We may not be able to use the gifts God gave us in ministry outside the home as often as we used to. This doesn't mean we necessarily stop serving within the church, but it may mean we reevaluate where we can and can't contribute. The gifts God gave us can be used right where we live for ministry in our homes and to our families.

Momming changes our identity too. Being a better mom is

not all about what we're doing. It is about who we are becoming in the process. In God's hands, the hard, sacred, and beautiful work of momming isn't robbing us; it is refining us. If we let him, God will use this time in our lives to move us closer to finding our identity—not only in being moms, but in Christ. That's why I love the apostle Paul's words: "Train yourself to be godly. For physical training is of some value, but godliness has value for all things, holding promise for both the present life and the life to come" (1 Timothy 4:7–8).

As moms, we are to be intentionally focused on pursuing Christ-like character. This is the ambition in life that matters most. We are to be ambitious for a transformed life that is marked by being like Jesus. As God changes us from the inside out, who we become will change what we do. Our pursuit of godliness will bear fruit in this present life and in the life to come.

Instead of us feeling like *less*, God can use the years of momming to make us *more* like Jesus. As we are shaping our children, God is using our children to shape us. He is teaching us to be awake to the fleeting time that he has so graciously given us. He is teaching us to count the days so we can make the days count (Psalm 90:12).

Following in the footsteps of Jesus is not easy. We all have a natural tendency to love ourselves first, promote ourselves, and comfort ourselves. This refining season of life shows us that we need to learn to love sacrificially and makes us more aware of the layers of self-indulgence we still have. Momming refines us by refocusing our eyes and hearts away from ourselves and the things we feel we've lost.

With all of its ups and downs, this season of life teaches us

The hard, sacred, and beautiful work of momming isn't robbing us; it is refining us.

that the mundane moments are never truly insignificant in his hands. This season won't last forever. Every person God has ever used and shaped has gone through different seasons too. Even Jesus experienced a season of refining and preparation.

RIGHT NOW IS NOT FOREVER

Have you ever noticed how we don't know much about Jesus's growing-up years? That is a season, for whatever reason, God doesn't tell us much about. But just because it was "hidden" doesn't mean it wasn't important.

Like most Jewish boys his age, Jesus was likely getting an education and learning a trade. He was attending synagogue, going to the temple, reciting prayers, making friends, and spending time with his family. Even for the Son of God it seems it was a rather quiet and ordinary season of life.

The last detail we learn about Jesus's childhood is, he "grew in wisdom and stature, and in favor with God and man" (Luke 2:52). After that? Silence. The Bible doesn't say a word about that season until Jesus bursts onto the scene in a very public fashion!

Long before Jesus did anything "noticeable" or "public," he was growing up. God the Father was raising and transforming his Son. God was using the season Jesus was in to prepare him for the season ahead.

What a great reminder for us as moms!

Jesus's season out of the limelight was not wasted time. A season of waiting on God is never a season wasted. And it's not less significant time. It's not robbing us of other, greater things. God uses the time and space of different seasons to teach us, refine us, and prepare us for future seasons. We are not "less" for being in this season; we are becoming more like Christ!

So guard against rushing through or overlooking the significance of the years of momming. Live with open hands and hearts to all God wants to do in you and through you. God is in the business of making us "more," not "less." He isn't robbing us. He is refining us.

CHAPTER 14

I Don't Know Who to Listen To!

I heard her yell long before I saw her. "M-o-o-o-o-m, can you help me?"

We were at one of our favorite playgrounds in Ann Arbor, enjoying dinner with some friends. We sat on a bench about fifty feet from the play area. We talked, ate, and kept a watchful eye on our kids as they played nearby. In the middle of our conversation, I heard it again: "M-o-o-o-o-m!"

Immediately, I recognized the voice as that of our youngest daughter, Sophia. This time her voice sounded more distressed. "I can't get down!"

I quickly turned my head in the direction of her cry, scanning what looked like a sea of kids playing on tractors and other farm-themed play equipment. Then I saw her. She had climbed to the top of a steel climbing dome—the kind that looks like a giant ball cut in half. She had scaled the summit all right. Getting up was not the problem; getting down was! She was hardly in any real danger, but she was sufficiently stuck at the top.

It always amazes me how we moms have a knack for hearing the voices of our children. It doesn't matter whether we are in a deep sleep in the middle of the night or at the playground with the loud voices of hundreds of kids swirling around us, the minute we hear our son or daughter's voice, we tune in. We know that voice is speaking to us, and it captures our full attention.

The problem is, it's not just our kid's voices we are good at picking up. We are also keenly dialed in to the voices of friends and relatives and the voices that come from church, social media, our culture, our past, our insecurities, and our fears. There is no shortage of voices, no shortage of people speaking their minds when it comes to momming.

Often these voices tell us what a mom should be, and more specifically, they tell us who we should be and what we should do as moms. These voices have the power to shape us—in the wrong way as well as the right way. With so many voices in the mix, it's easy to be persuaded, discouraged, confused, or even defeated. So who we listen to is incredibly important for influencing who we are becoming as moms.

SORTING OUT THE VOICES WE HEAR

Voices and the words they speak really matter. I recently witnessed the power of words spoken to a young mom who was desperately trying to get her child out of the cold and into a shopping mall. We saw her as we circled the parking lot—for the second time. It was two weeks before Christmas, which meant finding a parking space was about as urgent as finding presents.

Although it was an unusually sunny December day, that didn't take away the fact that it was a windy, biting twenty-six degrees.

Finally, we spotted a parking space and pulled in two cars down from a mom who was hurrying to get her child out of the car and into his stroller, out of the wind and cold. As we walked toward the mall entrance, we nearly caught up with her. We could see her efforts, and her frustration, as she tried to hold on to a diaper bag, push a stroller, and grab the warm blanket that had just blown off her young child.

And then we heard it—a woman's voice that sounded about as warm and friendly as the weather! The young mom and all of us looked to see an older woman who had just popped open her car door to deliver an urgent and important message.

"Where is that child's coat?" she yelled, noticeably concerned for the child. There was nothing subtle about her message. "You're a bad mom" came through loud and clear.

We had seen a flustered mom who was doing everything she could to keep her son warm and get inside when, forty feet from the entrance, his blanket had slipped off. The older woman did not see or understand what had happened, which led to her publicly shaming a young mom for being a "bad" mom. We all felt the embarrassment and pain this mom surely felt when she was already doing everything she could.

I think most moms have experienced similar moments. At the least, we've all had less-than-perfect momming moments that are more suited for blooper material than a highlight reel. We've all experienced a judgmental glance, an accusing question, a hurtful comment, or the right advice at the wrong time! It can be difficult to put those voices in perspective—to figure which ones we need to listen to and which ones we need to tune out.

Today there is no shortage of voices whispering in our ears, is there? It seems when it comes to momming, everyone has a voice—a message, an opinion, or a piece of advice. We have countless books, blogs, ministries, and social media channels offering how-tos and practical advice. We have well-meaning family members telling us how they used to do it. Friends without kids tell us how they would do it. And others, who are in the middle of doing it, eagerly pass along what works and what doesn't.

Some of this is good. Some of this is bad. Most of it leaves the average mom feeling like she has a placard around her neck saying, "Please help. I don't know what I am doing!" So what are some of these voices we hear as moms? Let me highlight a few.

The Voice of Failure

All of us have areas of our past we'd like to forget. Choices we made. Experiences we had. Sometimes our failures from the past still whisper to us today, causing us to feel unnecessary guilt or shame.

The Voice of Friends and Family

These voices, some of which are well-meaning, are voices of friends or relatives telling us how they parented. Because of these voices, momming can become a wild-goose chase to measure up to someone else's standards or expectations. The voice we often hear is, "I can't do it like them. They have it all together. I just don't measure up."

The Voice of Our Church

If we're honest, our church family can also be a voice that eats away at our hearts. A vision of biblical motherhood—which is so far out of reach without God's help—can cause moms to hide or pretend they have it all together. If we're not careful, church can become a place of judgment, self-righteousness, and guilt instead of encouragement, grace, and support.

The Voice of Our Culture

Our culture can send moms a message that they are missing out on "real life" while they are raising kids. We can be led to believe that momming is somewhat "less than" a "real" job. The voice can cause us to think, "I'm just a mom." Or "I wish I were doing something else, something more meaningful and important."

Moms also hear voices on social media. These are the voices that tend to make us believe everyone else is momming pretty close to perfectly. We get bombarded with pictures of vacations, crafts, Halloween costumes, spiritual milestones, and more. Very few moms share their worst momming moments with their Instagram followers or Facebook friends! The voice we often hear is, "She sure makes it look easy. I wish I could be as good of a mom as she is. I wish I had her life!"

It takes a careful ear to discern which voices we should, and shouldn't, listen to.

WHOSE VOICE REALLY MATTERS?

I remember being away at college and calling home frequently to talk to my parents. Whether it was during finals or when I was feeling homesick, I just needed to hear the voice of my mom or dad on the other end of the line. Theirs were the voices that mattered most. Just the sound of their voices comforted and encouraged me. Often they didn't use many words, but the sound of their loving voices was enough to keep me going.

But there is an even more important voice that speaks into my life and makes all the difference. That is the voice of God. He talks. He speaks often. And when you read the Bible, you notice pretty quickly that God brings life, beauty, and order to his creation by using his voice! Nine times in Genesis 1 the Bible records that "God said . . ."

"And God said, 'Let there be light'" (Genesis 1:3).

"And God said, 'Let there be a vault between the waters to separate water from water'" (Genesis 1:6).

"And God said, 'Let the water under the sky be gathered to one place'" (Genesis 1:9).

"Then God said, 'Let the land produce vegetation'" (Genesis 1:11).

"And God said, 'Let there be lights in the vault of the sky to separate the day from the night'" (Genesis 1:14).

"And God said, 'Let the water teem with living creatures'" (Genesis 1:20).

"And God said, 'Let the land produce living creatures'" (Genesis 1:24).

"Then God said, 'Let us make mankind in our image'" (Genesis 1:26).

"Then God said, 'I give you every seed-bearing plant'" (Genesis 1:29).

God's voice brings light! It drives out darkness! His voice creates order! When God speaks, his voice cultivates, nourishes, and produces new life.

And in the first three chapters of Genesis, we read that all of creation listens and responds to his voice. Light listened—the sun and moon took their places at God's command. The water separated. Vegetation came forth from the ground. The water teemed with new life. The land was pounced on by new and different living creatures. All of creation gladly responded to the sound of the Father's voice.

But early on in the Bible, we discover that God is not the only one who talks. And he is not the only one we listen to. Genesis 3 reveals that every person has a very real spiritual enemy, described in the Bible as a serpent. This snake is not any ordinary snake; it is our spiritual adversary, Satan. Genesis 3:1 records the first words that enemy spoke, in defiance of God's voice: "The serpent was more crafty than any of the wild animals the LORD God had made. He said to the woman, 'Did God really say, "You must not eat from any tree in the garden"?'"

What God says to us and about us helps us drown out the critical voices.

Not every voice we hear is from our spiritual enemy. But it's important to see how Satan can twist the truth and goodness of our Father's voice. Unlike God, Satan speaks lies, distorts the truth, casts doubts, tempts, and basically does anything he can to disrupt God's work and drown out God's voice. Sadly, his voice is sometimes louder than the voice of our loving and truthful Father. When we blow it as a mom, erupting in anger instead of patience, the voice of our enemy can leave us feeling guilty and condemned. Or maybe in a season when our children are doing well and we feel good about our parenting, we are tempted to take pride in our accomplishments as a mom.

Satan spoke through a serpent in the Garden, but he also uses many other voices today. These voices can even war against the truth of what it means to be a mom. He whispers and disguises his voice. But it's his voice nonetheless. The challenge for us as moms is to sift through all the wrong voices so we can clearly hear the voice of truth—the voice of our good, wise, and powerful Father. We want our hearts to be shaped by what we hear of *his* voice.

TUNING IN TO THE VOICE THAT MATTERS MOST

While there may be many voices we hear, there is only one that matters most: the voice of our Father who speaks to us through his Son, by his Word, in the power of his Spirit. God is still speaking to us today. And what he says to us and about us helps us drown out the critical voices. His voice has a way of shaping—and reshaping—our hearts. His voice nourishes our soul. It guides our steps. It focuses our minds and it steadies our hands for the hard work of momming. Consider how God's voice can guide us and ground us in our momming journeys.

God's voice reminds us we are loved.

While I was away from home during college, talking to my parents reminded me of who loved me the most. As moms, we need similar reminders. Momming is full of countless joys, but we get weary in the process. We can get beat up by momming. What grounds us is not when we see the fruits of our labor, get thanked for all we do, are respected, or fulfilled. What steadies our soul is that we are deeply loved by our Father because we are in Christ through faith. So the most important voice is the one that tells us we are perfectly loved and accepted in Christ. Galatians 3:26 reminds us we "are all children of God through faith." Henri Nouwen said it very well when he wrote, "Self-rejection is the greatest enemy of the spiritual life because it contradicts the sacred voice that calls us the 'Beloved.' Being the Beloved expresses the core truth of our existence."[8] God's perfect love drives out all fear (1 John 4:18) and any feelings that we are falling short or not measuring up. We need to remember that we are the "Beloved," fully accepted and cherished not because of our work as moms, but because of the work of Christ.

God's voice leads us without driving us.

People's voices drive us, telling us what a mom should be and do. Too often we get caught up in the whirlwind of voices and find ourselves being driven by fear, pride, or insecurity. We hear how a friend's child is already saying his or her ABCs. They are counting to twenty while our child is still trying to get to ten! Or maybe we learn that another family is sending their son or daughter to a sports or academic camp. The voices of other people have a way of driving us to do things. But trying to keep up with others is the wrong motivation. The voices of people that drive us can hurt our souls.

In contrast, Jesus is our Great Shepherd. He leads us, protects us, sustains us, and speaks to us. His voice is gentle. He says, "I am the good shepherd; I know my sheep and my sheep know me" (John 10:14). Jesus's voice leads us, bringing healing, wholeness, and hope to our hearts. He lovingly and patiently draws us closer to himself, to his righteousness, love, truth, and grace.

He reminds us that momming is not a race or a competition. Just as he is leading us, he is leading our children. We don't have to be anxious, fearful, or envious. The voice of Jesus speaks over us the approval that can only be found in him. We are secure in his love, confident in his truth, and hopeful in his promises. Even his voice of correction is spoken in love. His voice doesn't drive us but leads us as his love perfects us—making us better as we become more like Christ.

God's voice is perfecting us.

Often the voices around us tell us what we're not. The goodness and grace of God's voice is that he is always telling us who we are and puts before us the hope of who we are becoming (Philippians 1:6). Momming is not about perfection; momming is about being perfected. This process of being perfected is a lifelong process, one that will not be perfect or complete until Christ returns. Until then, God uses all the circumstances of momming to perfect us.

We are not always going to measure up. As good as we may be at times, we are never going to be perfect. We can't and won't always do it right. We'll make mistakes with our priorities, our words, our schedules, and our discipline. Our dream of being the world's greatest mom will get shattered—not once, but many times over.

We need to remember we are listening to the voice of Jesus. He's the only one with the spotless record. We are to tune our ears to him—the author and perfecter of our faith (Hebrews 12:2). He alone can help us when we are weak and humble us when we feel strong.

Just the other morning I crawled out of bed after a restless night of sleep cut short by Noah's growing pains in the middle of the night. I muttered a few unintelligible words to my husband and left our bedroom. Then staggered downstairs. After making a cup of coffee, I plopped on the couch. I was hemmed in by what felt like mountains of laundry—some on the couch and some on the floor next to my feet.

Within minutes of opening my computer, the alerts started to wake me up. Emails from blogs I subscribe to were popping up in my inbox. The social media notifications were adding up. My phone was chirping because of text messages I had missed overnight. Then flashing across the TV screen I saw: "Up Next . . . Five Habits for Cooking Healthy Family Meals." I was ready to go back to bed and pull the covers over my head!

So I turned it off. All of it. Clicked off the TV. Closed the computer. Put down the laundry. What I needed most, what my heart needed most, was to hear from God. I didn't need the voice of another blog. Nor did I need to hear how to cook a healthy meal. The text messages could wait. The laundry certainly wasn't going to run off! I needed to be alone in silence to hear the voice of God speaking to me through his Word.

Being perfected in momming means we make time with Jesus our first and greatest priority. We abide in his Word, grow in his grace, surrender to his love, and follow his example. We say goodbye to the many voices that don't speak the truth about who we are, who we are becoming, and what God has called us to.

We serve the God who speaks: our loving Father whose voice calls us into friendship, enabling us to move forward and onward. Listening to his voice settles us. It cultivates a heart that allows us to live the abundant life Jesus offers. So listen to his voice of love and truth—the voice that matters most.

CHAPTER 15

I Can't See Where I'm Going!

My phone buzzed with authority: *weather alert*!

"A weather alert?" I asked my friends. Another friend and I had stopped by a mutual friend's house to chat and hang out for a bit while our kids played together.

"I had no idea it was supposed to snow!" I said. "And not just snow . . . snow*storm*!" Before they could respond, their phones were buzzing too. Bad weather was heading our way.

Of course in Michigan we are used to bad weather in the winter, so we all shrugged off the warning and continued chatting. We were having a great time and paid little attention to what was brewing outside. But before we knew it, the weather hit. And it came down with fury. My kids and I scurried to the car and quickly slid into our seats so we could close the doors against the wind and snow swirling in every direction.

As we headed home it felt like we were hemmed in by

static—the kind of static on a TV channel when you can't get the picture to come in. What seemed like millions of white dots flashed and darted against the black sky. We could barely see ten feet in front of us. This was going to be a long and treacherous ride home.

My jaw was clenched. My fingers were wrapped so tightly around the steering wheel they hurt. Everyone was silent, too scared to talk. Except for me. As I searched for the lines on the road ahead, I comforted myself by saying quietly over and over, "Okay. Okay. Okay." We were only fifteen minutes from home ... in normal weather. But for forty-five minutes I searched desperately for signs that I was still on the road and deliberately kept my eyes focused on what I could see, not on what I couldn't.

I had never driven in conditions so awful and frightening. Thankfully, the headlights of oncoming cars, taillights of cars ahead, and the occasionally visible lines on the road revealed just enough to assure me that I wasn't in the middle of a snowy field. Slowly but surely, those markers guided me through the dense and blinding snow.

When I finally pulled into our driveway, we all sat in silence for a moment just taking in the terror we had just experienced. In that moment, our vision was restored. The weight was lifted. We felt such relief. We had made it home in one piece!

Sometimes momming feels a little like driving through a bad snowstorm. Endless needs and crises swirl around us like blinding static. One minute we feel we have it all together, and the next minute everything is falling apart. The house is clean and then within two minutes, it is a disaster again! Just when you utter the words "we haven't gotten sick in forever," the two-year-old gets the flu. Before long, the virus makes its way through the whole family, one child at a time. And just when you think all those parenting moments and teaching opportunities are finally sinking in, an epic explosion between siblings happens in the grocery store. Momming is a bumpy and scary ride, with moments when it is difficult to see the road ahead. Sometimes we're not even sure we're on the road!

What can help us see where we're going? What will keep us safe and on track during the storms of life? Having a clear picture of what God is doing makes all the difference. We need to keep our eyes focused on his purpose and mission for momming so that we do not become discouraged, disoriented, or perhaps, distracted from God's calling.

In the middle of the messiness of momming, we need to embrace the mission of momming. Just as the lines on the side of the road kept me on track when I couldn't see much of anything, a better understanding of God's mission for motherhood stands out like a marker and can keep us moving in the right direction. When the journey of momming was getting scary for me, a book from a dear friend was the marker that helped me to see more clearly.

EMBRACE THE MISSION, NOT THE MESS

I vividly remember standing in my living room with a newborn Noah in my arms, my toddler Bella clinging to my leg pleading with me to pick her up, and Tyler yelling from upstairs because he needed help in the bathroom. At that moment, I realized I was in way over my head. I was outnumbered. I wanted to be the best mom I could be so I tried and tried and tried. And the more I tried, the more overwhelmed I became. Honestly, I was blind to the route ahead because I was just trying to make it through each day.

Thankfully, the good Lord knew I needed a little help. Via a friend, he sent a very special gift to me. It was a book that would change everything. *The Mission of Motherhood* by Sally Clarkson opened my eyes to see that I didn't have to "just try to make it through the day" or "do the best I could." For the first time in my life, I saw there was way more to motherhood than I had realized. My motherhood journey wasn't just a hopeless, inescapable mess. It was indeed also full of meaning and purpose. God didn't make a mistake in choosing me to be the mother of my children. Instead, I could be confident he wanted to use me in their lives.

That is the message I want every mom to grasp. We have a mission, and it's right in front of us. God loves family: he loves *my* family and he loves *your* family. He created families, and he is using our families to help pass on faith, nurture and train children, and—ultimately—to reflect who Christ is to the world. Family is that good and important in God's eyes!

So momming is not just something we try to get through and hope to live to tell about it. Being a mom has a mission. We are not just raising good kids; we are raising disciples and followers of Jesus. Perhaps one of the greatest descriptions of the mission of family in general, and momming in particular, is found in Deuteronomy 6:4–7: "Hear, O Israel: The LORD our God, the LORD is one. Love the LORD your God with all your heart and with all your soul and with all your strength. These commandments that I give you today are to be on your hearts. Impress them on your children. Talk about them when you sit at home and when you walk along the road, when you lie down and when you get up."

As parents, we are to be the primary spiritual influences in our children's lives. All of life is God's classroom to teach, train, and live out God's truth. If you notice, verse six says God's truth is supposed to be in us before it's in our kids. We can't pass on what we don't possess. Our hearts are to be impressed, molded, and shaped by God's Word. And as God is shaping us, he is shaping our kids through us.

FOCUS ON THE MISSION

There is no shortage of ideas for how to raise children today. We get advice from friends or family members on what we should be doing with our kids. Our culture tells us what ought to be important to us and for our children. We may read different books or blogs, attend conferences, or listen to the radio—all giving the "right" image of what our families and children should be.

Pretty soon we are unsure whether we should be raising well-cultured kids who are involved in everything from French lessons to piano and dance or raising superstar athletes who are engaged in travel leagues, specialty camps, and clinics. Or maybe we should be aspiring to raise the academic overachiever who is focused on excellence and hard work in academics *and* extracurricular activities. Even church can be a confusing whirlwind of decisions about volunteering, Bible study, and of course, the choice to have your children attend home school, Christian school, or public school.

To find our way through the storm, we need to focus on the mission God has given us.

All of these competing pictures make it hard to find our way as moms. We're not sure of the direction we should be heading or how to get there. The static becomes blinding. If we don't know what our mission is, if we can't focus our sights on the lane markers, it's all just lots of advice, swirling like snow. Meanwhile, the mess of life with kids piles up all around us.

Yet God gives us markers, like lines on the road, that show us the way to stay on course, moment by moment. Driving in the snowstorm, I didn't need to see five hundred feet or a mile ahead of me. I just needed to know I was on the road and in a lane so that I could keep going in the right direction.

As moms we need the same thing. We need to focus on the mission God has given us in order to find our way through the storm. Otherwise, we'll be tempted to give up and embrace (or ignore) the mess instead of embracing the mission. But embracing the mission isn't always easy. Nothing important ever is, momming included.

THE REAL REASON MOMMING IS SO HARD

I don't know any mom who became a mom because she thought it was going to be easy. On the other hand, I don't know any mom who realized how hard motherhood was going to be! Momming isn't hard just because we're tired and bored, our kids are young and rambunctious, or because we don't know what we're doing. These reasons may be legitimate and, at times, true. But the real reason momming is hard is because motherhood is meaningful. There is a real purpose and mission for it. That mission, like every mission, comes with opposition.

Ultimately, the source of the opposition we face in the world is from our spiritual adversary—the devil. The Bible is clear that we have a real spiritual enemy who is on the prowl to distract, disrupt, distort, and even destroy God's work in the world. So while we need to be careful of giving Satan too much credit, we need to be careful of dismissing his presence and power completely.

We are engaged in a fight. We are waging war not only for our own spiritual maturity but for the hearts and minds of our children. Momming is hard because it is a spiritual battle. Notice how Satan seeks to oppose God's work: "Your enemy the devil prowls around like a roaring lion looking for someone to devour" (1 Peter 5:8).

But God does not only warn us of Satan's wiles, he also teaches us how to fight him:

- "Be alert and of sober mind.... Resist [the devil], standing firm in the faith" (1 Peter 5:8–9).
- "Finally, be strong in the Lord and in his mighty power. Put on the full armor of God, so that you can take your stand against the devil's schemes" (Ephesians 6:10–11).
- "Submit yourselves, then, to God. Resist the devil, and he will flee from you" (James 4:7).

Living out God's purpose and mission in momming requires us to stand firm, to resist the devil, to put on God's armor, to flee the devil, and to draw near to God. We are not momming alone. We have been given God's presence and power to fight the enemy because God's Spirit lives in us. There is no opposition we have faced, are facing, or will face, that we do not have the power to overcome with God on our side.

But the devil isn't the only source of opposition we face. The Bible says a lot about the opposition we face in the surrounding culture: "As for you, you were dead in your transgressions and sins, in which you used to live when you followed the ways of this world and of the ruler of the kingdom of the air, the spirit who is now at work in those who are disobedient. All of us also lived among them at one time, gratifying the cravings of our flesh and following its desires and thoughts. Like the rest, we were by nature deserving of wrath" (Ephesians 2:1–3).

The "world" in these verses refers to the institutions, values, and beliefs that are opposed to God. So the apostle Paul is contrasting an old way of living (before we were Christians) with a new way of living (as Christians). He's saying we used to be under the influence of the world's ways, beliefs, and values. But not anymore!

Unfortunately, some people take this to mean that everything in our culture is bad and evil. This is *not* what the Bible is saying! However, our culture is different from and often opposed to God's values. As moms who are called to live faithfully in the world, we have to learn to discern between God's values and the world's values. We need to be careful that we see our mission and purpose from God's perspective and not the world's. We need to be sure we measure our values against God's Word and not the world.

We might see these differences when we think about what our culture says about success, beauty, fame, or even true significance. For example, we can be persuaded to think that getting into the "right" school defines success for our kids. Sometimes the world values having the latest gadgets or the most fashionable and trendy clothing. Even good extracurricular activities can become all-consuming, replacing involvement in a local church or student ministry. All of these and more can appear innocent, or even desirous. But it takes wisdom, even courage at times, to allow God's values to define true significance, meaning, and success.

We also face opposition because of who we are. Even though we may be in Christ, and are seeking to follow him, we still struggle with who we used to be. There is still the presence of our "old life," the ways of the world that once dictated how we used to think, feel, and act. The power of sin may be gone, but the presence of our sin is still very real.

The New Testament often uses the word *flesh* to describe this. The Bible isn't talking about our skin; it's talking about our sin—all the ways we live separately from God because of our fallen and sinful natures. To live in the flesh is to live apart from God's resources that are ours in Christ. It is to live in resistance to our new relationship with the Father, through his Son, and the power of his Spirit. Our flesh can tempt us not to trust God, to be controlled by unhealthy emotions, and to allow our minds to be anxious or fearful. Our flesh can cause us to grow resentful, engage in gossip, explode in anger, and try to do the glorious but gut-wrenching work of momming in our own strength.

This is why throughout the New Testament we are encouraged and commanded to live by the Spirit and not by the flesh. For example, the apostle Paul says, "So I say, walk by the Spirit, and you will not gratify the desires of the flesh. For the flesh desires what is contrary to the Spirit, and the Spirit what is contrary to the flesh. They are in conflict with each other, so that you are not to do whatever you want" (Galatians 5:16–17).

When we are doing God's work, we should expect opposition. The different opposition we face as moms can war against our hearts, getting in the way of real and lasting change. Becoming who God wants us to be in this journey of momming can be obstructed by opposition, so it's important we know what it looks like. This will help us overcome these challenges and become who God wants us to be on this journey.

But we do not overcome the opposition on our own. We weren't made to. We were created to walk with God, breathing in his words and truth. We were created to walk with others, finding encouragement, strength, and protection by living in community with God's people. We were made to be filled, not with our own strength and wisdom, but with God's Spirit. The mission, and opposition, is too big to face alone!

The good news is that every opposition is an opportunity to be changed by God. This is the work of transformation. We are not just raising kids; God is raising us. And he is using the opposition we face in the mission of momming as an opportunity to shape us. And we're not the ones who schedule those opportunities on our calendars!

OPPOSITION IS OPPORTUNITY

I love being around people and want to be a part of everything. So as a new mom, I fought saying no! I wanted to be in the Bible study that I knew wouldn't work with my new schedule. I didn't want to give up serving in the same way I had been serving in our worship ministry at church. I wrestled with not being able to go and do what I wanted to do. As a new mom, all of it felt like opposition to my way and my plans. God gently reminded me it's not about me. It took a while to be at peace with my new season of momming and some of the limitations that can bring. But in saying no to some things, I soon learned I was saying yes to the ones who needed me the most.

Every opposition to living out God's purposes in momming is actually an opportunity from God to grow. To become better. To be made more and more into the image of Christ. Opposition is an opportunity either to persevere or to quit. Opposition is an opportunity to take the deep and hard look inward, uncovering the idols of our hearts. Opposition is an opportunity to humble ourselves and admit that the mess of momming is more than we can handle on our own. Opposition is the opportunity to die to ourselves—acknowledging that momming will not always satisfy our desires or meet our needs. But these opportunities help us depend on God in new and deepening ways, enabling us to increasingly love in selfless and sacrificial ways.

When we are seeking to be obedient to God's purposes and mission, we can be sure there will be opposition. That opposition comes not because of who we are or aren't as a mom, but because of who Christ is and who we are in him. But remember, where there is opposition, there is also great opportunity for God to continue shaping us into the image of Christ. Momming is not just what we are doing; it is who we and our children are becoming. The purpose and mission of momming is the stuff of eternity. So when the "snow" starts to fall, and it gets difficult to see where you're going, keep your eyes focused on what matters most: your mission!

CHAPTER 16

I Need Some Alone Time

H ow many?" the hostess asked.

"Just two of us tonight," we said, a bit giddy. I almost felt guilty for saying it with such enthusiasm. Normally we ask for a table for six, which always generates a look of concern from the host or hostess. But not tonight. Just the two of us were dining out—without the kids!

"Follow me," she said, walking us toward a covered patio near the back of one of our favorite Italian restaurants. Spotting the table she was taking us to, I couldn't help but notice the group seated at the next table. I quickly did the math—five kids plus six adults equals—eleven?

A table of eleven? I thought to myself. My husband and I exchanged glances, not saying a word. Our "alone time" was not going to be nearly as alone as we had hoped. We were away from our kids, but we were not going to be away from someone else's kids!

For couples with children, it can be a struggle to find time for "just the two of us." Finding alone time with kids in the house is as rare as having a clean house. And sometimes, as we learned that night in the restaurant, we're not away even when we finally get away!

It is no less challenging for a mom to find the time and space she needs to be alone. As busy as life often gets, our moments of alone time will become less and less frequent if we don't make it a priority. We're busy taxiing kids to school, practices, activities, and friends. We're making meals, filling drinks, and cleaning up after spilled ones. We're doing laundry, changing diapers, and a whole lot more!

Now that my kids are getting older, most of them sleep in later (can I get a hallelujah and an amen?!), which means my best chance for time alone is usually before they wake up. So I sneak out of bed, walk quietly downstairs, and head straight for my biggest morn-ing motivator—the coffee maker. But even those early morning moments are sometimes invaded by an early-morning intruder.

It's not easy to find time alone, but we need it. To be at peace, our hearts require time to be alone. But it's not enough to simply get away from the kids for some peace and quiet. What our hearts need most is time carved out to meet with God. We need time for just the two of us to be together. As God is shaping us through the experience of momming, we need time to hear from him and talk to him about who we are becoming. We need to make time for God not because he needs it, but because *we* need it.

MAKING A PLACE FOR GOD

Several years ago I was roped into trying to read the Bible in ninety days. I say "roped" not because I didn't want to do it or because I thought it was a bad idea, but because I suspected it would be nearly impossible for a busy mom. But I eventually decided to give it my best shot.

I read fast. Sometimes, while making dinner, I listened to the audio version on my phone. I read far more than I could comprehend, and I need to confess that I skimmed—okay, skipped—some parts too. I hate to admit it, but in some parts I really struggled to see the value or connection of what I read to "real life."

However, I did love it at first. I was all in as I read the stories of God's people crying out in their slavery and God graciously hearing their prayers and delivering them from Egypt. It was exciting to read about the miraculous crossing of the Red Sea and their venture into the desert in what would become a long walk to the land of promise.

Then I hit chapter twenty-five of Exodus. Then chapters twenty-six, twenty-seven, twenty-eight, twenty-nine—all the way to chapter forty! For almost fifteen chapters Moses goes on and on describing the tabernacle, God's tent, the place his presence would dwell while his people journeyed through the wilderness. To me, that seemed like too many chapters to spend on the tabernacle. That's when I began skimming. Until I hit this verse in the last chapter of Exodus: "Then the cloud covered the tent of meeting, and the glory of the LORD filled the tabernacle" (Exodus 40:34).

What?! Suddenly all the descriptions and instructions made more sense to me. I hadn't understood why Moses spent so much time describing the tabernacle until I read how God's presence filled the space when it was all done. Then I got it! It took work and skill to build a space suitable for God to fill. Only after God's people made room for him—then and only then—did God fill it with his presence.

This has been an important reminder for me as I struggle to carve out space from my busy life to meet with God. Almost fifteen chapters of Exodus were dedicated to making sure we know God is completely holy and also desires to be with us. God delights in being with his people. He wants to be close to us and wants to live among us. But he leaves it to us to create the time and space to be with him.

Yes, it is true that God's presence is everywhere. In Christ, God's Spirit dwells within us. He is with us when we're wrestling with our kids. He is there when we are doing the dishes. God is present around the table as we tell stories about our days. There is no space that God does not fill with his presence. But God knew that the people he had freed from slavery in Egypt needed a tabernacle as they journeyed through the wilderness and learned to become his people. So there is a sense in which the tabernacle was not built for God, but to be a holy space set aside where God's people could meet with him.

Just as the Israelites needed a tabernacle to meet with God, share life in his presence, and discover what it means to become his people, we need a "tabernacle" too. We need space in our lives that is set apart for meeting with God, sharing life with him, and discovering how to become who God desires us to be. But finding this time and space will not come easy for busy mommas!

We need to make time for God not because he needs it, but because we need it.

Sometimes it takes sneaking out of bed early to enjoy a cup of coffee and some alone time with God. Other times we have to carve out space during our lunch hour at work, when the kids are at school, out playing, or down for a nap. Our "tabernacle" may not always look the same. But no matter how full of hurry and hustle our days may be, we need to make room and create space to meet with God.

Even Jesus withdrew from the busyness of life to be alone with his Father. I love Luke's description: "At daybreak, Jesus went out to a solitary place. The people were looking for him and when they came to where he was, they tried to keep him from leaving them" (Luke 4:42).

Jesus, arguably the busiest man on earth, knew the value of solitary places where just he and God could enjoy their relationship together. He, too, had to work to carve out space. He, too, had his alone time invaded by "people looking for him"! Time alone with God doesn't always come easily, and it doesn't always last long. But we need to be diligent in making room for God so that he fills our "space" in order to teach, correct, encourage, and shape us into the image of his Son, Jesus. Just as Israel needed to make a place for a transformational relationship with God, we need to make a place for that same kind of relationship.

BEING WITH GOD TO BECOME LIKE JESUS

It would be nice if God would wave a magic wand so we would instantly become the better moms we want to be. But God rarely changes us by "zapping" us. We don't go from being anxious and fearful moms one minute to being filled with peace and contentment the next. We don't become better moms—moms who exhibit Christ-like character as we go about our daily lives—by working hard at doing just the right things to "fix" our sin and brokenness. When we recognize our shortcomings and want to become better, our first response should not be, "I'll try harder." It should be, "Lord, I need you. I want to spend time with you."

If we want to become more like Jesus, our first priority should not be what we are *doing* to be like him, it should be simply being *with* him. We set aside time and space to share a relationship with God because being with him inevitably makes us more like him. Think about it for a minute. You probably know people who change you when you spend time with them. Perhaps you have a friend who, no matter how bad a day you are having, leaves you feeling comforted or calmed just because you have spent time with her. Other people may leave different marks—perhaps a sense of peace, courage, or strength. It might sound strange because we don't often think of it this way, but the same thing is true of our alone time with God.

We don't start becoming like Jesus by trying to be like him. Instead, we start by spending time with him. No matter how hard we try, time alone won't transform our hearts. Time alone with God will. When we open our Bibles to read, we're really open-ing our ears to hear him. When we memorize Scripture, we are soaking in God's truth and grace. When we pray, fast, or journal, we are opening our hearts to an intimate and transformational relationship with him. Over time, that relationship changes us because God's Spirit is at work in us. By spending time with God, we take in his love, grace, and truth like little seeds. The water of a relationship over time produces a crop in our lives that is increasingly more like Jesus—full of love, joy, peace, patience, kindness, goodness, and self-control.

I love the language Jesus uses in John 15:4 when he says, "Remain in me, as I also remain in you. No branch can bear fruit by itself; it must remain in the vine. Neither can you bear fruit unless you remain in me." Jesus doesn't just tell us to obey his commands; Jesus invites us into communion. An abiding and life-transforming relationship that changes us over time.

What is essential in this picture of abiding is relationship. We were made for communion with God. We are not simply following an idea or a set of religious beliefs. God is alive and well! We are in relationship with a real being who is present and powerfully active in our lives. Our growth and maturity, our becoming better, more like Jesus, is a by-product of that relationship.

When we make room for God, he meets us in that sacred space. God meets us and speaks to us through his Word, by his Spirit, and in the company of his people. We open our hearts to hear from God, receiving more and more of his love, truth, and grace. God is not just working *on* us; he is working *with* us. A difference that is easy to understand as a parent.

WORKING WITH GOD TO ACCOMPLISH HIS PURPOSE

Any mom who has ever tried to help her child do homework knows the joy and agony of working with her children. I have the math gene in our family, so who gets to help with math assignments? You guessed it. It's a good thing I like numbers and that math comes easily for me because not all of our kids excel at it.

Working with my children to help them understand and apply their math skills is not easy. I can't just tell them what to do and assume the lesson is done. We have to work together. As they seek to learn and grow, I seek to help them understand. We have to communicate with one another to make sure we are on the same page before progress can be made. It all gets harder, more time-consuming, and more confusing once you hit the algebra years. As fun as math can be, we have had our share of "math meltdowns." To be more precise, these are not just meltdowns, they are more like shutdowns. Cooperation between teacher and student ceases to exist and forward progress stops!

In momming, we are not just working *on* our kids, we are working *with* them. Working with them requires their cooperation. This is not only true in math; it's true in every area of life. As much as we hope they receive our love and guidance, we know they are free to resist or reject it.

It is also true of us as we grow up in Christ and become better moms. God does not force his way on us. He delights in us as his children: "The Spirit himself testifies with our spirit that we are God's children" (Romans 8:16). He pursues us and hopes we will receive his love and guidance, but the work of God's Spirit in us is not coerced. God has started a good work and he will finish it. But God does not just work *on* us, he works *with* us, and that requires us to work with him to accomplish his purposes in us.

As I have strived to carve out space to meet with God, draw close to him, and follow where he leads, I have found it helpful to ask questions about areas of my life in which I may be working against what he wants. It helps me cooperate with what he wants to do in me when I have taken time to understand what becoming like Jesus looks like in my life.

Our oldest son recently started working for the first time, and every time I dropped him off for work, I felt the weeds of anxiety creeping into my heart. I'd think about who he is working with. Are they being nice to him? I'd wonder what kind of influence he was around. And then I would stop myself, asking my heart the difficult, but important question, "Am I *trusting* God or trying to *be* God?" The answer to my question revealed how, once again, I was working against God instead of working with him. Trying to be God was keeping me from enjoying the joy and peace God has for me when I trust that he is parenting my son.

This is not the only question I am learning to ask myself. Sometimes in a moment of frustration or anger, I need to stop and ask, "What selfish desire is controlling my heart right now?" And sometimes at the end of the day, I ask the scary question, "Where did I fall short today? Where did I sin against God, my spouse, or my kids?" These questions are not always easy, but with God's help, they do expose the places of our hearts that need God's healing, forgiveness, or truth.

Like a parent who lovingly wants to see us grow up and walk in the truth, God is working with us. He is not done with you, and he is not done with me. He is working with us, shaping us, and making us more like his Son as we shape our children. More than just asking us to be like him, God is inviting us to come be with him. To meet with him. Know him. Learn to love and be loved by him.

As is true in any relationship, this can't be done from a distance. God wants to draw near. Will you draw near to him? Will you carve out room to meet with him? Will you use your alone time to be alone with God?

CHAPTER 17

I Don't Have Enough Time Left

The kids were finally in bed, and my husband and I were looking forward to a little romantic time for ourselves. We knew as it got later the chance that both of us would stay awake was growing slimmer. So we headed upstairs. Quietly, of course, so we didn't wake the kids.

My husband was feverishly brushing his teeth. I was going through my normal nightly routine of removing makeup, washing my face, and brushing my teeth. My "prep" time apparently was too much for my husband. Sounding slightly annoyed, he finally commented, "Honey, are you going to wash your face all night?"

As I looked up to respond to his attempt to speed things along, he noticed something else. "Are you crying?" he asked.

Not even the water was able to hide the redness in my eyes or the struggle I was having in my heart. He asked again, "What in the world? Why are you crying?"

He didn't know it, but I had been wrestling with an issue with our oldest daughter, Bella. She was heading into eighth grade, and I was torn about what to do for school the following year. We had always said we would take schooling decisions one year at a time, and that was fine when the kids were in first or second grade. But now each year was becoming more and more critical. She was moving toward high school far too quickly for my comfort, and I didn't want to make a mistake.

Although we had talked about it over dinner earlier in the week, I had said little about how torn I continued to feel about the upcoming decision. We both knew the window of opportunity, the window of influence we would have as parents, was closing quickly. And the question of which schooling option would be best for her remained unsettled in my mind.

My husband rightfully reminded me that making a decision at 11:00 at night was probably not the most strategic, healthy—or romantic. Instead of enjoying time with my husband, I was obsessing over momming. *I don't have enough time left with Bella!* I thought. *I have so much I want to teach her yet!*

ALL TOO BRIEF

Needless to say, that night did not end as we planned. And I'm a little embarrassed now at how I let momming get in the way of nurturing my marriage (it's one of the reasons we wrote a whole book on the subject—*For Better or For Kids*). It illustrates, however, how every mom longs to make the most of her all-too-brief mothering years.

Yes, the time God gives us with our children matters. While it is true we always have some influence on our kids—even when they are grown up and move out of the house—the time they spend living with us is unique and passes quickly. God is always shaping us, but as moms we will not always have the same opportunity to be shaping our kids. So we both want and need to be wise stewards of the tiny moments, minutes, and hours we have. Because this is a holy time.

I, for example, can be a stickler about going to bed with a clean kitchen. I'll wipe down the counters. Put away dishes. Straighten chairs around the table. But if I am not careful, my semi obsession with a clean kitchen can steal away precious moments from my kids. In a year, or ten years, will it matter that I had a clean kitchen before I went to bed? I seriously doubt it! But the impact of those quiet—okay, sometimes hectic—moments before bed with my kids will last forever. We all need to slow down and make sure we remember what matters most when momming is messy. We need to take the time we have with our kids seriously, before it's gone. Which is a lesson God had to teach his people from the very beginning of the Bible.

TAKE THIS TIME SERIOUSLY

It's always been interesting to me that the first place in the Bible God uses the word *holy* is in relationship to a day—in relationship to time: "Then God blessed the seventh day and made it holy, because on it he rested from all the work of creating that he had done" (Genesis 2:3).

He was setting aside a period of time to help his people rest and know when to let God be God. They needed to be reminded that time was not only set apart *from work*, but set apart *for God*. Time is holy—sacred—and we honor the sacredness of time by the way we use it.

When we use our time for God, we use it well. I love Psalm 90:12: "Teach us to number our days, that we may gain a heart of wisdom." The Hebrew word for "wisdom" is really the word for "skilled." And let's face it, we don't always use our time skillfully or wisely. We can let one evening of "vegging out" watching TV turn into a family habit. We can allow social media to be a convenient distraction from meaningful conversations in the car or at home. Even good activities can crowd out the priority and practice of spending time together as a family in God's Word, serving in our church, or building much-needed community.

It takes skill to steward our time well. It's something we have to learn. We need to seek God and ask for his help in learning how to steward our time in a way that makes our days count. The apostle Paul reminds us of how important this is: "Be very careful, then, how you live—not as unwise but as wise, making the most of every opportunity, because the days are evil" (Ephesians 5:15–16).

Time will eventually take our kids to new seasons—seasons like dating, college, marriage, and careers. It may take them to new places, new towns, different states, or faraway countries. We cannot stop time, but we can and must steward our time. Today is the day to be "very careful" and make the "most of every opportunity" so that we use our time for God's purposes.

Time is not our enemy. While it is often sobering to think about the future and the fleeting time we have, this is why we are raising our kids! We're not raising our kids to keep them. We are raising our kids to release them to God for his purposes. Which is sometimes a hard pill for a mom to swallow, especially when you are snuggling on the couch with your youngest.

RAISING OUR KIDS TO RELEASE OUR KIDS

I was quite cozy, snuggling with two of our kids on the couch, when our five-year-old daughter said to me, "I'm never going to leave you, Momma! I'm going to live next door forever!" As sweet as her promise was, I was pretty sure she would change her mind by about age ten! But admittedly, I secretly wished she would stay close.

Some days we want to keep our kids forever, and other days, well, it seems appealing to release them! Release, for example, sounds like a good idea around dinnertime, when they are all circling the kitchen like a flock of seagulls. But for most moms, *release* is a bad word that leaves us with a scary feeling.

When our oldest son recently announced that he wants to go to college in California, everything inside of me wanted to blurt out, "No, you can't do that! That's too far away!" For a moment I comforted myself with the realization that his announcement may have been motivated by the fact we live in Michigan and it was winter. Whether or not college in California actually happens, it is scary that his days of walking a college campus are only a few years away. This time matters. I'll be releasing him sooner than I would like. How can I make this time really count?

God calls us to be obedient today and to trust him for tomorrow.

The whole idea of making the most of the days and moments we have raising our kids before we release them into the world can be overwhelming. I find encouragement in the example of Jesus who called his disciples to himself for a purpose: "He appointed twelve that they might be with him and that he might send them out to preach" (Mark 3:14).

Did you catch that? Jesus called twelve of his disciples to be with him that he might send them. Jesus would be present with them, purposefully preparing them to be sent out. In all that Jesus did, he was intentional and strategic with the time he had. He knew he was raising his disciples to be released.

Just as Jesus taught his disciples, we look for everyday opportunities to teach and train our kids to follow God's Word in God's world. Just as Jesus was patient with his disciples, we show grace to our kids as they grow toward maturity. We pray with them and for them. We plant God's truth in them, helping them to memorize and reflect on God's promises. And just as Jesus modeled a life aligned with God's priorities, we let our example impress on our children the goodness and blessing of walking with God.

God has given us each of our kids for a greater purpose than just being our son or daughter. Each one is God's own child and will be his forever. As God shapes us, he is shaping them. He is using us to raise them, so that like arrows, they will be released to penetrate the darkness of the world.

As moms, we don't need to be fearful about tomorrow, but we do need to be faithful today. The seeds we plant today—the sacred moments we use skillfully each day—when watered by God, will bear fruit tomorrow. I was reminded of this on a recent trip we took down memory lane.

WHAT WE DO TODAY MATTERS TOMORROW

It had been several years since we had seen the house we lived in when we brought each of our four kids home from the hospital.

We had moved, so it was rare for us to have a reason to pass by our former home. But when we had the opportunity, we thought it would be fun to drive by the old, turn-of-the-century house we had loved so much.

Well, *I* had loved that house. For my husband, that house represented a lot of work. You name it, we did it. New carpet. New paint in every room. Eventually we purchased new appliances. And the list goes on. We also completely redid the landscaping with the help of a neighbor who told us what to plant and where to plant it.

While we didn't get to go into the house, we drove several times around the block to get a good look on the outside. And to our amazement, the tiny trees we had planted now shaded the backyard. Bushes that were barely big enough to see when we planted them now looked like they needed to be trimmed back. Flowers were in full bloom. Ferns had multiplied and now covered the whole side yard.

What started as a small and humble landscape design was now flourishing. There was an abundance of vegetation. Lots of color. And new life that had been planted and nurtured by homeowners who came after us. It was a work we well remembered starting, but never expected to see to completion.

Isn't that like the calling we have embarked on as moms? We plant seeds. We water them. We pray for God's protection. We work and work, never knowing whether we'll see the full fruit of our labor. Like the gardener, we faithfully and patiently work today for the sake of what will be produced tomorrow.

We plant seeds and do the work of gardening as we live daily by example. We cultivate life with each conversation. We open the Scriptures, telling the stories of what God has done and will do, as we quietly hope and pray that the seeds will take root. We get our hands dirty, digging in the dirt of our kids' hearts, imparting new life with the help of God's Spirit. All of it is hard work. It is slow, and sometimes thankless, work. But ultimately, it is God's work.

We won't always see the outcomes of our faithfulness. God calls us to be obedient today and to trust him for tomorrow. Our time counts. We need to steward it well. What we do today matters for tomorrow. But it's not only what we do, it's who we are becoming that will influence our kids tomorrow.

SHARING OUR LIVES WHILE GOD SHAPES OUR LIVES

The apostle Paul shares a wonderful thought: "Because we loved you so much, we were delighted to share with you not only the gospel of God but our lives as well" (1 Thessalonians 2:8). He was writing to a church, saying in essence, "I didn't just love you from a distance. I didn't just preach a sermon from a platform. I didn't just know you from afar. But I loved you up close and personal. I knew you and you knew me." This is why he says that he was delighted to share not only the Word, but his life.

Isn't this so true of momming? We don't parent from a distance. We share our lives with our families. Our kids get to see who we really are, up close and personal. They don't see who we project to the world. They don't see who we think we are or sometimes pretend we are. Our kids see us as we are. We know them and they know us. This can be really good—and really scary!

The truth is, while God is graciously shaping us and making us more like Christ, who our kids are becoming is largely influenced by who we are becoming. This time matters because we have the power to influence our kids not only by what we say or do, but by who we are. They are watching how we handle conflict. Deal with loss. React to authority. Serve a neighbor. Love our spouse. In countless ways, they see how our hearts are unfolding and responding to God's grace and truth that transforms us. So many times we are shaping our kids based on what God is first doing in us.

It is true we are saved by grace. And God works through our brokenness and shortcomings. It is true we will never be perfect. Only God *determines* who our kids become, but we do *influence* who our kids become. God invites us to become better, more like Jesus, because little hearts and minds are being shaped every day. The power of our influence is great in God's hands. With God's help, we want to be able to say as Paul did, "Follow my example, as I follow the example of Christ" (1 Corinthians 11:1). While we will never have "enough" time, we will always have "enough" of Christ, shaping us, forming us, and influencing us so we can in turn shape our children.

CHAPTER 18

I Want to Make a Difference

'*ve always loved to work. As early as I can remember, I helped my dad in his home office. He was a small business owner, and I helped with some of the paperwork and record-keeping. I'd sort files, make copies, stuff boxes, and answer the phones. Even though I was young at the time, I can still remember the joy I experienced from working. It wasn't just having a job and making some money that I enjoyed, it was the fact I was contributing—adding value to the work my father did.

As much as I loved the feeling of working hard, the real satisfaction came from the sense that I had helped to accomplish something bigger than myself. It's been decades since I worked in my dad's office, but my desire to make a difference is as strong as ever. I want to contribute. I want to leave my mark in this world. So it wasn't easy for me almost fifteen years ago when this deep, internal desire ran head on into being a mom.

I dove into being the best mom I could be. I loved momming.

I loved my kids, cared for them, served them, taught them, and gave them a loving and secure environment to grow up in. I knew that by being the best mom I could be I was making a difference, adding value, and contributing to my children's lives and our life as a family in countless ways. All of these things—my love for being a mom, caring for and making a difference in the lives of our kids—are still true. But at the time I struggled with making a difference *only* as a mom.

By *only* I don't mean that the work of momming is somehow less than any other work we may do. It's not. There is no such thing as being *just* a mom. The *only* I was struggling with was that I didn't want to make a difference as a mom and be unable to contribute in other ways as well. It seemed to me that God had called and gifted me in many different ways, and I wanted to use those gifts in significant ways too.

I know many moms share in this struggle. Obviously, there are seasons when it isn't the right time for anything other than being a mom. But many of us still can't deny our longing to make a difference in something that is much bigger than ourselves. So let me share a well-known secret with you. The truth is, God has created each of us to make a difference, not only in momming, but in other ways too.

CREATED TO MAKE A DIFFERENCE

If you are feeling that gnawing desire to contribute in the world outside of your role as a mom, you are not alone. In fact, if you have to put the "blame" anywhere, put it on God. He made us this way! We weren't created just to exist; we were created with ambition, godly ambition.

The very first book of the Bible tells us about God's power and purpose in creation. God made us to live for something bigger than ourselves: "So God created mankind in his own image, in the image of God he created them; male and female he created them. God blessed them and said to them, 'Be fruitful and increase in number; fill the earth and subdue it. Rule over the fish in the sea and the birds in the sky and over every living creature that moves on the ground'" (Genesis 1:27–28).

We were made to live for God! He created and shaped us for accomplishment. He gave us authority to rule the earth in partnership with him. He gave us a mission to represent him in the world so the world would know what he is like. No wonder we want to live for something more. God has shaped and molded us in his image so we can go out and change the world!

As we become more like Jesus, who is the "image of the invisible God" (Colossians 1:15), we show the world the truth, beauty, power, and love of God. We are to be ambitious, living for the good of the world and for God's glory. If that sounds lofty, it is! The good news is there are lots of different ways we can make a difference. For me, it was starting a blog.

MAKING A DIFFERENCE, NOT *ONLY* AS A MOM

I had dabbled with a few jobs here and there as I looked for ways to satisfy that yearning to make a difference. I had always had a heart for women, especially moms, but I never dreamed I would be led to make a difference by starting an online ministry. I was, however, intrigued by the blogs I read for moms—blogs about cooking, parenting, homeschooling, and more. The more I read, the more I found moms from all walks of life.

That is when it hit me. I wanted an online space to bring moms of different ages and in different stages of life together to create a community where we could all learn from one another and grow together. So, in 2012, I started *The Better Mom* (www. thebettermom.com). And wow! With a small dream and a lot of desire to make a difference, God has done far more than I ever imagined!

The first month my site was live, I was stunned when we hit ten thousand visits. I thought that was as big as it would get. Boy, was I wrong! Each month the community grew larger and larger. Today, there are nearly half a million moms and women who learn together and encourage one another through the ministry of *The Better Mom*.

We're all wired for work—the kind of work that makes a difference in the world for God's glory. We're doing that as moms, but momming is not the *only* place we can make a difference. God gives us desires and opportunities in other ways too. For me it was starting a blog—a little online corner where moms across the world could come together to learn and grow.

But work looks different for each of us. For some of us it might look like involvement in a ministry at church, in the community, or in a parachurch organization. For a mom who works outside the home, it may look like listening and praying for a coworker or pursuing a career that changes the world for the better. It may be offering godly counsel for a friend or neighbor going through difficult times. It may be opening your home to others. It might look like doing ministry *as* a family instead of just focusing on ministry *to* your family.

God has wired us and called us to serve him in different areas and with different gifts. So there is a good reason we often feel the desire to make a difference as moms and in ways other than momming. Whatever we do, he has called us, equipped us, and sends us out to make a difference in the world. This is true whether you are a stay-at-home mom, work-from-home mom, or work-outside-of-the-home mom.

But there is a right time too. Just like there are different seasons in life, there are different seasons in momming.

IT'S ALL A MATTER OF TIMING

One of the things we love about living in the Midwest is the different seasons. Spring is full of cooler but comfortable temperatures. In summer, we enjoy the heat and full sun that enables everything to grow and flourish. Fall is for football. And the trees show off their vibrant colors as we cool down from summer. Winter is cold but beautiful with plenty of snow. Winter always has a way of slowing us down. We love each of these seasons and have learned that each season is uniquely different. I have often thought that momming has its seasons too.

We go through different seasons that are beautiful, but challenging in their own ways. Different seasons call for different actions. Newborn babies require intense one-on-one nurturing. Toddlers require a keen eye and steady discipline. School-age children soak up everything we can teach them. Teens need our support, advice, and counsel. While each season has its limitations, each season also has its opportunities. Even Jesus experienced different seasons. His life and ability to accomplish the mission his Father had called him to required that he be guided by "divine time." He had to be sure his timing was also the Father's timing. A great example of this is found in John 7.

Jesus was in Galilee, but it was almost time for one of the large festivals the Jewish people celebrated, called the Festival of Tabernacles. The location for this joyous celebration was the city of Jerusalem. If Jesus had been looking to "grow a platform" or increase his following, it would have been an ideal time to make a public move to reveal who he really was—the Messiah.

In God's way and in God's timing, go make a difference!

Public recognition was probably the motivation of Jesus's half-brothers, who were trying to convince him to go to Jerusalem. Ironically, they didn't yet believe he was the Messiah, but they couldn't help but notice the timing. Notice what they said to Jesus: "Leave Galilee and go to Judea, so that your disciples there may see the works you do. No one who wants to become a public figure acts in secret. Since you are doing these things, show yourself to the world" (John 7:3–4).

They were urging Jesus to go public! You need to "show yourself to the world," they said.

I love (and often need to remember) what Jesus said in response. In several short verses, he reminded them that obeying God's timing is also a part of obeying God's commandments. He said, "My time is not yet here" (verse 6) and then again, "My time has not yet fully come" (verse 8).

Jesus would eventually make himself known, but not yet. Not right now. Not in the way his brothers wanted him to. Jesus would publicly and prophetically make his way into Jerusalem to let the world know he was the Lamb of God. Every eye would see the One who had come to take away the sins of the world through his life, death, and resurrection.

For Jesus, the timing was just as important as the task. His mission was motivated by God's timing and not his. While there are many important truths in this passage, Jesus's timing and understanding of different seasons is applicable for momming. Every season is important. Every season is different. But there are certain seasons that limit what we can and cannot do.

A NEW SEASON WILL COME

The early seasons of momming are incredibly tough. The season when kids aren't sleeping through the night, when it seems like every other month a sickness sweeps through the house, and when just trying to keep everyone alive and fed is all-consuming. During that season there were times when I longed to contribute in different ways. I wasn't using gifts and abilities I knew I had.

But God was telling me "not yet." God had to whisper in my ear, "You are already making a difference. This is my mission for you today. But it's not my only mission for you. Be patient. Keep growing. Trust me and don't grow weary."

No one else may notice what you are doing and no one may applaud the faithfulness being formed. But these "secret" seasons of life are not less important than any other season. We're not missing out if we are in a tough momming season that requires everything we have to give. But I promise you there will come a time when the seasons will change, when things will be different. And when that new season comes, be ready to step out in faith.

No matter what season of momming we find ourselves in,

God is always at work (John 5:17). He's at work in the small stuff. The big stuff. The neat stuff. The messy stuff. It's his story and we have the joy of participating in it in countless ways—in some ways we see and probably many ways we don't. God is at work and he invites us to do something, but not everything.

God has wired us to make a difference—as moms, but not *only* as moms. It's okay to long for more, because we were wired for more. First and foremost, God is using us in the lives of our children and that *is* something—something big. But when the time is right, there may be something else God calls you to do. In God's way and in God's timing, go make a difference! You were made to.

CHAPTER 19

I Want to Enjoy the Journey

My mother-in-law was a wife and mother who loved and served God even when it wasn't easy. She had been through a lot during the nearly fifty years of marriage she and her husband shared before he passed away. They had been in ministry for several decades, raised three kids, experienced the loss of a newborn child, and then started and operated several home daycares.

In her later years she was light-hearted, wise, and godly. Her years of ministry and momming gave her a perspective I didn't always have. I was curious how she did it. So not too long after my father-in-law passed away I asked her, "What would you do differently?" I wanted to know what she would have done if she had the chance to be a young mom again. I wanted to know what advice she would give herself as a young wife and mother who was struggling to keep it all together.

Her answer was likely one you've heard before. After pausing for just a moment, she said, "I would have enjoyed the journey."

She answered that question more than five years ago and has since passed away. Meanwhile, much has happened in our lives. We've moved to a new city to start a new church. We've changed homes. Our kids have grown older. One is almost half-way through high school, which means he will soon be out of the house. But I have not forgotten my mother-in-law's simple response: "Enjoy the journey."

It's not as easy to do as it sounds. When we are in the middle of the mess of mothering children, it can be tough to truly embrace and enjoy where we are. It's tempting to get so caught up in the day-to-day challenges, stresses—and, of course, joys—of mom-ming that we can't see beyond the moment.

Yet through it all, God is growing us, one step at a time. We may not yet be who God wants us to be, but we are not who we used to be. We are not who we were when we took our first steps as wives and moms. As we continue to shape and influence our kids, we can be sure God has a plan and that it encompasses even the most difficult or seemingly insignificant details of our lives. He is going to finish what he started in us (Philippians 1:6), and that alone gives us much to be thankful for—even when it's not easy. Which, once again, God had to remind me of on a recent Saturday night.

Our kids had been playing at our neighborhood playground when one of them came bursting through the front door. "Tyler hurt his leg!" our daughter frantically announced. We had been getting ready to call them home, as it was getting late, and it was time to start getting ready for church the next morning.

"It looks really bad, Mom!" she added. Really bad can mean a lot of different things to a protective mom like myself. Our oldest son came limping through the door. And then I saw it. My daughter was right!

His shin looked like someone had taken a baseball bat and swung for center field! The rapidly swelling lump on his leg looked about the size of a softball.

Calm, cool, and collected would have been the appropriate response when I first saw his leg. Not that night. Shock, confusion, anger, and panic would be a good way to summarize what was swirling around in my head.

Moments after he came through the door, I had him on the couch, icing his leg. As it turns out, he had slipped while climbing on a jungle gym, slamming his shin on one of the metal bars. Between questions of how, when, why, and where this happened, I was feverishly scanning articles on the internet for what a broken leg looks like. So much for a quiet and restful Saturday night before church in the morning. It was looking like a trip to the hospital or urgent care.

Fortunately, after some time and lots of ice, his leg was looking better. The swelling went down drastically, as did my anxiety! As the clock moved closer to midnight, I found myself breathing a huge sigh of relief. Another messy moment. Lots of tears. Circumstances I would not have chosen. But I was thankful.

I wish I could always stay calm when I find myself in the middle of a messy moment. But there have been countless tears, heartaches, and words spoken out of anger. But regardless of the season or the circumstances, I am learning to be thankful. I am learning to be thankful for the messes, loads of laundry, noisy car rides, walks in the park, conversations over dinner, and yes, even the close encounters with illnesses or injuries. *All of it*—because all of it is changing me.

In a letter he wrote to a group of Christians, the apostle Paul gives us an important key for learning how to become thankful when the journey is difficult: "Just as you received Christ Jesus as Lord, continue to live your lives in him, rooted and built up in him, strengthened in the faith as you were taught, and overflowing with thankfulness" (Colossians 2:6–7).

Jesus invites us to come to him as we are, but we are not to stay as we are. We are to live our lives "rooted and built up" in Christ. He is the one who strengthens us in faith. He is the one who gives us joy for the journey. Paul says a person who continues to be rooted in Christ is not just to be thankful but "overflowing with thankfulness." And that's a person who has learned how to enjoy the journey.

Paul further clarifies that we are to "give thanks in all circumstances" (1 Thessalonians 5:18). How is this possible? We can be thankful because circumstances are not by chance. Sick kids. Homework that was supposed to be turned in. Another unexpected car repair. Nothing in our lives comes to us without first passing through God's loving hands. God is using every circumstance to shape us. Change us. Grow us up and grow us closer to him. Who we are becoming through our life circumstances matters because those around us are watching.

WHY IT ALL MATTERS

Stephen was an early follower of Jesus whose love for Jesus cost him his life. In a confrontation with some of the Jewish religious leaders, he shared why Jesus was the Messiah, God's Savior. The confrontation didn't go well, or so it seemed. When Stephen got toward the end of his passionate sermon, the religious leaders covered their ears, yelled, and dragged him out of the city to his death.

I don't think that turn of events was on Stephen's to-do list that day. It wasn't exactly a positive and encouraging response to his faithfulness to the responsibilities God had given him! But there is an important detail in this story: as Stephen was being stoned, "the witnesses laid their coats at the feet of a young man named Saul" (Acts 7:58).

If we stopped reading the Bible at this point, we'd miss why this detail is so significant. However, several chapters later, this "young man named Saul" encounters Jesus in a powerful and life-changing way.

Saul had been a faithful Jew who was known for persecuting the church. After meeting Jesus, he became known as one who was growing the church! By his grace, God did a great work in and through Saul (who later changed his name to Paul). So what does this have to do with Stephen? I think, a lot!

Saul was a "witness" to Stephen's faithfulness. He was so close to the action that the witnesses laid their coats "at his feet." He was close enough to hear Stephen. Saul watched him. Perhaps he even joined in with the crowds opposing him. This story is a great reminder that we are in close proximity with people every day who may not yet be following Jesus. While only God can change someone's heart, like Stephen, we can live as faithful witnesses for who God is and what he has done. We may never know the full impact our lives may have on those around us, or at what point someone will come to know Jesus through saving faith. All God asks us to do is to be faithful. He takes cares of the rest! We are in close proximity with people every day who don't yet know Jesus. We are called to be faithful in the everyday and allow him to work through us, whether we see the results or not. We never know when they will accept Christ. While only God can change someone's heart, he asks us to be faithful witnesses for him, and we need to trust he will use us.

We all have "Sauls" in our lives. People who watch us. Listen to us. Know us. Are influenced by us. Our "Sauls" are our own sons and daughters. We have the privilege of influencing them for better or for worse. Often influence happens in small, "insignificant" moments that might easily be overlooked. So every part of this journey matters not only because of what God is doing in us, but because of what God is doing in the people around us.

Momming matters. By God's grace, the kind of moms we are becoming—in the crucible of our best days and our worst—is shaping the generations to come after us. This is why I started and love the ministry of *The Better Mom*.

Over the years I have received countless emails and heard many stories of how God has worked in the lives of moms. One particular email that landed in my inbox over three years ago left quite an impact on me.

In this letter, a mom chronicled her life. She began by sharing her life story, which had been anything but easy. But she was blessed to marry someone who she thought was perfect for her. As the years went by and they started a family, her world began to crumble. She felt disconnected from her children, who were entering their teen years. She and her husband weren't on the same page spiritually or in their parenting, and she felt the distance between them growing. Her spiritual life was falling apart. And the list goes on.

But then she stumbled across my website, TheBetterMom. com, and began faithfully reading the encouraging blogs from our contributors every single day. She shared how God was using those articles to change her in a myriad of ways. As her story continued, I noticed something changing. She began to share how she and her husband were spending more time together, how her relationship with her children was healing, and how her family was evolving before her very eyes. After all of this, she concluded her letter in this way:

> My point is this: I prayed for God to "help me."
>
> I believe He guided me to your writings. Your pieces hit so many places about being a mom and what a blessing it is to have my babies in my life and, as a result, you have greatly impacted Chelsea, Matthew, Justin, and Emily in a way that you may never even realize, but I wanted to say thank you just the same because I realize what your work has done for us as a family.

Tears streamed down my face as I read her words. You see, she got it. The change in her life had nothing to do with me and everything to do with her. God was changing her. In what had felt like hopeless circumstances, God reached in and was changing her as she learned to cling to him.

Who this mom was becoming mattered, not only for herself but for her entire family. It didn't happen overnight. There was no magical moment. Becoming better was not a giant leap into perfection. Who she was becoming was the result of steady steps of faith, walking closely with Jesus.

INTENTIONAL AND HOPEFUL STEPS

My youngest daughter, Sophia, taught me some important lessons about following in the footsteps of Jesus in the middle of a snowstorm.

We had to go out, but it was snowing and there were already several inches of fresh snow on the ground. As we looked at the unshoveled sidewalk, my daughter said to me, "I'll step into your footprints, Mom." So out the door we went.

I hadn't taken more than five steps when I heard her voice, "Mom, you are walking too far apart. Take smaller steps so I can stay in your feet."

Isn't that what it is like to follow in the footsteps of Jesus? One step at a time he invites us to follow him. Sometimes the steps are a stretch and we have to call out for his help. But with each step he calls us to become better. He doesn't run ahead of us, but he does stay out in front of us. He is patient, walking slowly enough so we can walk "in his feet," but persistent enough that we keep moving forward.

God loves us far too much to allow us to stay where we are. Instead, he invites us, one step at a time, into something better. He leads us out of an old life and into a new life. Jesus is leading and loving us every step of the way. He doesn't get too far ahead of us to make following him and becoming like him impossible.

Enjoy the journey. Be thankful for where you are. And rejoice over how far you've come.

I don't want to idealize being the perfect mom, nor do I want to glorify being a bad mom. But by God's grace, we can be intentional moms who are moving toward becoming better moms. We're not just wanting to become better at what we do but better by becoming more like Christ. As we are shaping and influencing our kids, God is shaping us.

The good news is, God is not done with us. What he has started, he will complete. So enjoy the journey. Be thankful for where you are. Rejoice over how far you've come. Keep walking, one step at a time with hope and confidence in who you are becoming: a better mom.

Notes

1. Collicutt, Joanna. *The Psychology of Christian Character Formation* (London: SCM Press, 2015), 114.
2. Nouwen, Henri. *Life of the Beloved: Spiritual Living in a Secular World.* (New York: Crossroad, 1992), 33.
3. Lewis, C. S. *A Grief Observed* (New York: HarperCollins, 1994), 72.
4. Buechner, Frederick. *The Hungering Dark* (New York: HarperOne, 1985), 73.
5. Lane, Timothy. *Conflict: A Redemptive Opportunity.* (Greensboro, N.C.: New Growth Press, 2006), 5–6.
6. Zacharias, Ravi. *The Grand Weaver: How God Shapes Us Through the Events of Our Lives.* (Grand Rapids, Mich.: Zondervan, 2006), 43.
7. Stanley, Andy (@AndyStanley). Twitter, April 17, 2013.
8. Nouwen, Henri. *Life of the Beloved: Spiritual Living in a Secular World.* (New York: Crossroad, 1992), 33.

For Better or for Kids

A Vow to Love Your Spouse with Kids in the House

Patrick and Ruth Schwenk

The transition from "married" to "married with children" can be tough. Less sleep. Tighter budget. Busier schedule. As much as you love your children and work hard to nurture and train them for the future, the challenges that come with parenthood can make the "for better or for worse" promise a hard one to honor.

With biblical wisdom and practical help, husband and wife team Patrick and Ruth Schwenk will inspire you to:

- build a God-centered marriage instead of a child-centered or me-centered marriage
- avoid the dangers of spouse neglect and self-neglect
- effectively communicate in the chaos
- explore ways to parent together as one team
- find balance in the busyness

For Better or For Kids is about remembering that children may join you in marriage, but they don't have to come between you! We can make a vow to love our spouse with kids in the house.

Hoodwinked

Ten Myths Moms Believe & Why We All Need To Knock It Off

Karen Ehman and Ruth Schwenk

PSST...want to know the secret for being a great mom?

Think she keeps house like June Cleaver, cooks like a Food Network star, and actually *does* all of the things she pins to her Pinterest boards? Oh ... and all while calmly raising her kids *without* ever raising her voice? *Yeah ... right.*

Karen Ehman and Ruth Schwenk have had enough of these misconceptions. Myths such as: "The way I mother is the right (and only) way," "Motherhood is natural, easy, and instinctive," or "My child's bad choice means I'm a bad mom." These myths leave moms hoodwinked and sometimes even heartbroken.

In their straightforward yet encouraging "we've been there" style, Karen and Ruth enable mothers to:

- identify the ten myths of motherhood
- replace the lies with the truth of what God says
- forge healthy, supportive relationships with other moms of all ages and stages
- confidently embrace the calling of motherhood as they care for their families in their own unique way

Ultimately, *Hoodwinked* equips mothers to stop searching for the secret and instead to develop and embrace their relationships—with their kids, other mothers, and, most important, with God.

A six-session video Bible study for group or individual use is also available.

Available in stores and online!

Pressing Pause

100 Quiet Moments for Moms to Meet with Jesus

Karen Ehman and Ruth Schwenk

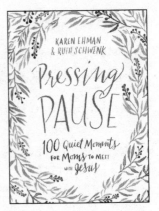

Kids bickering? Schedule jam-packed? Dishes and laundry both piled up high? Perhaps it's time you pressed pause.

Whether you're juggling a career, kids' schedules, and church commitments, or you're covered in spit-up and anxious about what the next eighteen years might hold, you can carve out a few quiet moments to rejuvenate your spirit.

Pressing Pause offers you a calm way to start your day, to refresh yourself in Jesus, and drink deeply of His presence so that you are ready to pour out love, time, and energy into the people who matter most to you.

These 100 encouraging devotions for moms will help you begin each day with Scripture, drawing on God's power, ingesting His Word, and learning practical ways to love and serve more like His Son.

Just a few minutes each day can help you center your heart and mind on what God has for you as His beloved daughter. So resist the rush. Halt the hustle. Press pause and find some calm in the chaos.

Available in stores and online!

thebetterMom.com

It is just incredible that you have taken the time to read these pages and seek wisdom as you grow in this journey of motherhood. I would love nothing more than to continue to be an encouragement to you in the future.

If you are looking for a community to connect with other moms, *The Better Mom* is the place for you!

At *The Better Mom*, our mission is to build God-honoring homes by inspiring moms to be better moms through sharing life and learning together.

I believe God has placed a high calling on our lives as we: raise children to impact the world, take care of our homes, love our husbands, and ultimately honor God with our lives.

I would love to have you join our community and share in our journey!

Join in with us!

the better Mom

PODCAST

WITH
RUTH SCHWENK

Tune in to The Better Mom podcast with Ruth Schwenk
and friends, as we gather together, grow as women, and
in turn give the best of who we are to our families!